ALL-INCLUSIVENESS
and UNLIMITEDNESS of
C H R I S T

Witness Lee

Living Stream Ministry
Anaheim, California

First Edition, February 1999.

ISBN 0-7363-0475-4

Published by

Living Stream Ministry
2431 W. La Palma Ave., Anaheim, CA 92801 U.S.A.
P. O. Box 2121, Anaheim, CA 92814 U.S.A.

Printed in the United States of America

99 00 01 02 03 04 / 9 8 7 6 5 4 3 2 1

CONTENTS

PREFACE

This book is a translation of messages given by Brother Witness Lee in a conference held in Taipei on October 27 through November 3, 1984. These messages were not reviewed by the speaker.

CHAPTER ONE

IN WHAT HE IS

Scripture Reading: Exo. 3:2-6, 14-15; John 8:24, 28, 58; 1:1, 14; 1 Tim. 3:16; Heb. 2:14a; Col. 2:9; John 19:5-6; Heb. 2:9; Col. 1:20; 2 Cor. 5:21; Rom. 8:3; 1 John 1:7; Heb. 9:12; John 12:24

OUTLINE

I. Jehovah God in eternity—the Creator:
   A. The self-existing and ever-existing Jehovah—the eternal, great I Am—Exo. 3:14; John 8:24, 28, 58.
   B. The Triune God—the God of Abraham, the God of Isaac, and the God of Jacob—Exo. 3:15.
   C. The Angel of Jehovah, the Triune God—Exo. 3:2-6.
II. A man of blood and flesh in time—a creature:
   A. Being the complete God who became flesh, possessing the complete divine nature—John 1:1, 14; 1 Tim. 3:16.
   B. Being a man of blood and flesh who was born of blood and flesh, possessing the perfect human nature—Heb. 2:14a.
   C. Being One who is both God and man—a God-man—a mingling of the divine nature with the human nature, without a third nature being produced.
   D. Being the embodiment of the fullness of the Godhead of the complete God—Col. 2:9.
III. The sin-bearing God-man in His vicarious death—the Redeemer:
   A. As the One who is both God and man, passing

through death in His humanity with His divinity—John 19:5-6.

B. As a created man, bearing man's sins and dying for every created thing—Heb. 2:9; Col. 1:20.

C. As a man of flesh, being made sin on behalf of man and condemning sin in the flesh—2 Cor. 5:21; Rom. 8:3.

D. The blood that was shed being the blood of Jesus (humanity), the Son of God (divinity), and being the blood of a genuine man with the eternal and unlimited efficacy of God—1 John 1:7.

E. Being the eternal (unlimited) Redeemer who accomplished an eternal (unlimited) redemption—Heb. 9:12.

F. Being the divine grain which passed through death to bring forth many grains—John 12:24.

We thank and praise the Lord that by His sovereign grace we can have another time together. In this conference we want to see the all-inclusiveness and unlimitedness of Christ.

CHRIST BEING ALL-INCLUSIVE AND UNLIMITED

As we all know, the center of the Bible is Christ. The universe is a mystery, and God is even more a mystery. According to the biblical revelation, God as a mystery hinges entirely on Christ. Yet, who is Christ? What does Christ involve? This is truly hard to explain thoroughly with human words. In the sixty-six books of the Bible there are at least three to four hundred ways of depicting the all-inclusiveness and unlimitedness of Christ. What He is, is so much and so limitless. That is why even though the Bible uses sixty-six books to depict Him, it still cannot describe Him fully.

The Bible portrays Christ with different types, figures, representations, stories, and even with different people, plants, animals, and items in nature. Many readers of the Bible often view it as a religious writing. They think that since religion is a system in which there is an object of worship with a corresponding set of teachings, the Bible must be a book that teaches people according to the One they worship. I dare not say that this concept is altogether absent in the Bible. However, there is only very little of it, and it occupies a very secondary position. What the Bible primarily does is to reveal Christ, that is, to show us and to explain, illustrate, and narrate to us who Christ is and what Christ involves.

We know that in human history no one is more excellent or more mysterious than Christ. He is not only real but also living. He is now; He still lives today. In the past two thousand years, human history has never been able to separate itself from Christ, for Christ is the turning point in human history. We all are brothers and sisters here. Thank the Lord that we are the blessed ones. We all have been saved and regenerated, and we have a union in life with Him. We have a heart to love Him and also to pursue Him. Every day we pray to Him and have fellowship with Him. Every day we regard His supremacy, and we desire to express Him in our body regardless of our circumstances. Therefore, in the Lord's recovery today what we need most is to know this Christ. Even though this topic seems old, I believe that every point and every item which we will point out will be as new and fresh as the morning dew. May the Lord give us grace and bring us into such a deep and fresh knowledge of Christ.

When speaking about Christ, whether it be in what He is, in what He has accomplished, in His person, in His work, or in any other aspect, the Bible always shows us that He is all-inclusive and infinite. Concerning His all-inclusiveness, He includes God and man, and He includes you and me. He includes eternity past and eternity future. He includes yesterday, today, and even tomorrow. He is truly all-inclusive, and at the same time, He is also unlimited. To be unlimited means to be without beginning or end, limitless, boundless. The biblical revelations concerning Christ cannot depart from this point; that is, everything pertaining to Christ is all-inclusive and unlimited. Therefore, in these messages we will specifically consider the all-inclusiveness and unlimitedness of Christ. Because time is short, there is no way to include many messages. We can include only five messages, but each message will contain many crucial points, every one of which is a mystery. I hope that you will do your "homework" diligently by following the outline and verses with each message. I also hope that within the year you will have a thorough understanding of the all-inclusiveness and unlimitedness of Christ and be able to speak it convincingly. When you speak, there should be no need to refer to the notes. Rather, you should be able to open your mouth and speak as a river flowing endlessly to testify wonderfully on behalf of Christ.

THREE ASPECTS OF CHRIST

From all the revelations in the Scriptures, we can see that there are three great aspects of Christ. These three great aspects are easy to remember. The first aspect is that Christ is God. To be sure, as God, He is all-inclusive and infinite. The second aspect is that Christ is man. Christ is God, yet He is also man. You may ask what is all-inclusive about man. Even a large man may weigh only two hundred and fifty pounds. Even after you have graduated from a university or have obtained a doctorate degree, your stature has not increased by much. Man is neither all-inclusive nor infinite. A man may be strong, but can he work vigorously for twenty-four hours a day? After working vigorously for only four hours, he may collapse. Man is not infinite; rather, man is finite. However, as a man, Christ is infinite. Christ is infinite not only as God but also as a man. Perhaps we never dreamed that there is a man in human history who is both infinite and all-inclusive.

③ The final aspect is that Christ is the Redeemer. He is God, He is man, and He is our Redeemer. The title *Redeemer* in Chinese is literally the "saving-redeeming Lord." Hence, it includes three things: saving, redeeming, and Lord. Never consider that *saving* and *redeeming* are the same thing. Saving is one thing, and redeeming is another thing. He saves, He redeems, and He is the Lord. He has saved and redeemed us; consequently, He truly is our Lord.

Christians are familiar with the term *Redeemer,* but they do not know why this term is used. How can Christ save us, and how can He redeem us? Moreover, why do we need to be saved and redeemed? Many of you are young ones who may have been saved for only three or five years. The church in Taipei has a history of thirty-five years, and I am eighty years old this year. When we first established the church here, the parents of some of you, the younger ones, were not yet married. I am very glad to see that in the church today many young brothers and sisters love the Lord very much. In my service to the Lord for over fifty years, I feel that particularly in these last two to three years, both in the West and in the East, the condition of the ones who love the Lord is unprecedented; there are many who love Him. Recently I stayed for six days in Tokyo, Japan. I saw in the meetings that over eighty percent were young people. I also stayed in Seoul, South Korea for six days. I saw that almost a thousand people attended the meetings, and the majority were young people. I was very joyful to see so many young people loving the Lord. That is why I have a heavy burden to fellowship with you, without reservation, everything that I have dug out from the Bible and everything that I have enjoyed and experienced in these few decades.

After I seriously prayed and sought the Lord in His presence concerning the general subject and the outlines for these messages, the Lord told me that I should speak about His all-inclusiveness and unlimitedness. Therefore, the general subject of these messages is the all-inclusiveness and unlimitedness of Christ. The burden for these messages can be summarized by the following five statements: 1) In Christ dwells all the fullness of the Godhead bodily; 2) The riches of Christ are unsearchable; 3) His breadth, length, height, and depth are boundless; 4) He is the One who fills all in all; and 5) He gives the Spirit without measure. The Spirit is the realization and transfiguration of Christ. Thus, Christ gives the Spirit, who is Himself, without measure. He is all-inclusive and unlimited, and now He has been transfigured to become the Spirit to reach us and dispense Himself into us without measure.

We need to remember these three crucial points: He is God; He is man; and He is the Redeemer, the saving-redeeming Lord. There have been many great people in history, including thinkers, statesmen, philosophers, and others. Although everyone has the boldness to say that he is a man, can you find one who dared to say that he was God? As human beings, we are finite, yet Christ as a man is infinite. Moreover, who throughout history dared to say that he could save and redeem us and that he was the Lord? It is very interesting that when people accept nearly any religion, they almost never say that they believe in the founder of their religion as the Lord. Only the gospel preaching of Christianity tells people that to believe in Christ is to believe in Him as Lord. This is because Christ is Lord. There is no other Lord who saves in this universe; only He is Lord. Let us shout over and over that Christ is God, man, and the saving-redeeming Lord! Is it not wonderful to believe in the Lord? Are you not happy to believe in Him? Have you been deceived, or did you suffer a loss to believe in Him? No, you did not. You must say, "This is a real bargain!" Our believing in Jesus is truly a bargain. If today you spend one dollar to buy a diamond that is worth ten million dollars, is that not a bargain? However, to believe in Jesus is so much more of a bargain than this. Who is Jesus? He is God, man, and the Redeemer. Is it not wonderful that we can receive Him simply by calling on Him? Once you confess your sins and believe in Jesus, you can receive Him. Whom do you receive? You receive Christ as God, man, and the saving-redeeming Lord.

I. JEHOVAH GOD IN ETERNITY—THE CREATOR

As we have said, the general subject of these messages is the all-inclusiveness and unlimitedness of Christ. The first message is on what He is, that is, on His person. We have already covered what He is in three aspects—God, man, and the Redeemer. First, we will look at the aspect of Christ's being God; this is an aspect in eternity. What is eternity? Eternity is the eternity past which cannot be traced in time, a past which is without beginning, without measure, and without limit. Therefore, in eternity, that is, in eternity past, in the infinity before time, Christ was Jehovah God. He was God, whose name was Jehovah. This God is the source of all things in the universe. He is the Creator, and all things were created by Him. When He created, He did not make something out of existing materials. Rather, He created something out of nothing; that is, He created all things out of nothing. Hence, He is the Creator, the source, of all things.

This Creator is God. The Hebrew word for God is *Elohim.* The word *Elohim,* a compound noun made up of two words, means "the faithful, mighty One." He is the mighty One with power. Moreover, He is the mighty One who keeps His promise. Elohim God is the faithful, mighty One, whose name is Jehovah.

A. The Self-existing and Ever-existing Jehovah—
the Eternal Great I Am

The title *Jehovah* is also a Hebrew word which is basically the same as the verb *to be.* The name *Jehovah* simply means "to be." What does this mean? This means that this faithful, mighty One is the One who is. In the universe, only He is, and all the rest are not. The phrase "to be" equals "to exist." He exists; hence, He is. If He did not exist, He would not be. The name *Jehovah* is "to be," and this "to be" is without beginning or ending. Hence, the Chinese version of the Bible renders this name as "He who is self-existing and ever-existing." To be self-existent is to be without beginning, and to be ever-existing is to be without ending. His being, His existence, is without beginning and without ending. This Creator is self-existing and ever-existing.

A wooden podium exists and has being, but we cannot guarantee that it will be here in forty or fifty years' time; it will not continue to exist here forever. After fifty years, we cannot say where it will be. In other words, soon it will no longer be or exist. Someone may have a lovely cat at home, but it can live at most for a little over ten years; after that, it will not be or exist. Therefore, its name cannot be "To be." It is the same with us human beings. Our human life span is the limit of our existence. If our life span is one hundred years, then we will exist for one hundred years. We can celebrate the new year only one hundred times, not one hundred and one. After one hundred years, we will not exist and be no more. Hence, our name cannot be called "Jehovah"; we can only be called "Not-Jehovah." The name Jehovah means "To be," but our name is "Not to be." *Jehovah* means *to exist,* but our name is "Non-existence." The name *Jehovah* means *to be present,* but our name is "Not present."

The Chinese version of Revelation 1:4 speaks of Him who exists now, who existed in the past, and who will exist in the future. In Hebrew, Jehovah means *He was, He is, and He is to be.* That is why He is trustworthy. He is not only the faithful, mighty One but also the ever-existing, mighty One. Therefore, the Lord Jesus told the Pharisees in John 8:24, "Unless you believe that I am, you will die in your sins." Who can save us? Only "I Am" can save us. Who is "I Am"? "I Am" is Jehovah. In the name *Jesus, Je-* is the simplified form of *Jehovah* and *-sus* means *Savior.* The name *Jesus* means *Jehovah the Savior.* The One who is self-existing, ever-existing, without beginning, without ending, ever-living, ever-being, and ever-present has come to be our Savior. This is the meaning of the name Jesus.

Then, we may ask Him, "Lord, You said that You are, but what are You?" The Lord would say, "I am whatever you want, and I am whatever you lack. What do you want? Do you want life? Good, I am life." We may say, "Lord, I want salvation," and He would say, "That is right. I am salvation." A brother may say, "Lord, I cannot love my wife." The Lord would say, "That is wonderful! I am love." Then the sisters may say, "Not only can the husbands not love, but we, the wives, also cannot submit. Lord, Your Bible tells us to submit. What shall we do? Therefore, we want submission." The Lord would say, "I am submission." The young people may say, "It is such a hardship for us students to study. I want to pass the entrance examination into a good school. Therefore, I need wisdom." The Lord would say, "That is wonderful! My name is Jehovah. I am your wisdom and intelligence."

We thank the Lord that He is! In John 8, the Lord mentioned three times that He is "I Am" (vv. 24, 28, 58). In verse 24 He says, "Unless you believe that I am, you will die in your sins," and in verse 28 He says, "When you lift up the Son of Man, then you will know that I am." The Lord seemed to be saying, "The day that you lift Me up on the cross to kill Me, you will be happy because you will think that you have won the victory by terminating Me. Little do you know that I always am; I can never be terminated! When you kill Me, apparently I am dead, but actually I am alive. By killing Me, you give Me an opportunity to live. Eventually, I will live and come out of Hades and the grave." This is what the Lord meant when He spoke this word in John 8. On the day the Jews crucified the Lord Jesus, they would know that this Jesus is Jehovah, the I Am who is self-existing and ever-existing.

Among the Jews, at least Saul of Tarsus was one who was like this. The Jews had already killed the Lord Jesus, yet Saul still continued to destroy the church and persecute the believers of Jesus. However, on his way to Damascus, the Jesus whom he persecuted appeared to him from heaven and said to him, "Saul, Saul, why are you persecuting Me?" (Acts 9:4). Saul was shocked, and he must have thought, "I persecuted Stephen, but when did I persecute someone who is from heaven?" Therefore, he asked, "Who are You, Lord?" The Lord said, "I am Jesus, whom you persecute" (v. 5). Only then did

Saul realize that this Jesus was Jehovah, the I Am whom his fathers worshipped. That is why, in effect, the Lord said, "After you have crucified Me, you will know that I am. If you do not kill Me, you will not know that I am the I Am. I cannot be killed. The more you kill Me, the more I live. Your killing Me will instead result in My coming to live in you." In the end, we can only bow our head in worship and say, "Lord Jesus, now I know that You are. You really are." We thank and praise the Lord for this.

B. The Triune God—the God of Abraham, the God of Isaac, and the God of Jacob

Furthermore, this God is of three aspects. He is the God of Abraham, the God of Isaac, and the God of Jacob. This title clearly shows us God in His three aspects. The God of Abraham is God the Father, the God of Isaac is God the Son, and the God of Jacob is God the Spirit. Jacob was a hard case, but God the Spirit came specifically to deal with such hard cases. In his entire life, Jacob was under the transforming work of God the Spirit, and eventually, he became Israel, the prince of God.

The Triune God is just one God. God is one, yet He has the aspect of three: the Father, the Son, and the Spirit. The Father is the Planner, the Designer, and the One who purposed. The Son is the Accomplisher and the Finisher, and the Spirit is the Executor. The Father is the source, the Son is the course, and the Spirit is the flow. The Father came forth in the Son to accomplish what He had planned, and the Son, after accomplishing everything, came into us as the life-giving Spirit. Therefore, God is triune that He may enter into us to be our enjoyment. This One whom we enjoy as the Triune God is all-inclusive and unlimited. When we enjoy Him, we enjoy both His all-inclusiveness and unlimitedness. We all have to know Him to such an extent.

C. The Angel of Jehovah, the Triune God

This Jehovah who is self-existing and ever-existing, the Triune God, also came to be an Angel, a sent One. He Himself came to be His own sent One. This Angel of Jehovah, this One who was sent by Jehovah, was the Triune God Himself. We have to understand that this One is our Lord Jesus. On the one hand, Exodus 3 is very simple with only a few verses concerning Him, but on the other hand, these verses are all-inclusive. He is self-existing and ever-existing, He is the I Am, and He is God. He is also the God of Abraham, the God of Isaac, and the God of Jacob—the Triune God. Finally, He is His own Angel. These are the aspects of Christ as God.

II. A MAN OF BLOOD AND FLESH IN TIME—A CREATURE

Another aspect of what Christ is, is that He is man. As God, He is related to us not directly but indirectly. Two thousand years after He created man, He came to tell Abraham, "Abraham, I will cause you to have a seed who will be a blessing to the nations." Who was this seed? Paul told us later that this seed was Jesus Christ. Matthew 1:1 says, "Jesus Christ, the son of David, the son of Abraham." This son of Abraham is Christ. After the promise was given, another two thousand years passed, and when human history fully reached four thousand years, He came. How did He come? It is marvelous that He is the Father, the Son, and the Spirit, and the Spirit is for reaching man; when He reached man, He came as the Spirit. The Holy Spirit came upon an unmarried woman, a pure virgin named Mary. He entered into the womb of this virgin and was conceived there. This almighty God, the Triune God, the Lord who is self-existing and ever-existing, the eternal Lord, entered into the womb of a little virgin for His conception, and He remained in the womb for nine months. He was there fully abiding by the natural laws that He had ordained in creation. According to the natural laws set up by Him, human conception must take nine months, so He waited there for nine months. Then He was born of the virgin to become a man of blood and flesh. This man had a nose, eyes, skin, flesh, bones, and blood. To be sure, He was a man, but this man possessed not only the human nature but also the divine nature. The conception of Christ was a mingling of two natures, divinity and humanity. Therefore, the elements within Him were divinity mingled with humanity. For this reason, Isaiah 9:6 says that the child born in the manger was the mighty God. This One was the God-man, who was both God and man and who was God yet man.

A. Being the Complete God Who Became Flesh, Possessing the Complete Divine Nature

This God who was conceived in humanity is not a partial God but the complete God, the Triune God—the Father, the Son, and the Spirit. We Christians often have a wrong natural concept, thinking that the Lord Jesus became flesh as the Son of God only. You must know that there is no such statement in the entire New Testament. The New Testament says that in the beginning was the Word, the Word was with God, the Word was God, and the Word became flesh. Thus, the Word is not a partial God, but the complete God. He was not God the Son only; rather, He was God the complete Triune God—God the Father, God the Son, and God the Spirit. Therefore, He possessed the complete divine nature. This is why Paul said in Romans 9:5 that Christ is God over all, blessed forever. Our Lord Jesus is not the Son of God only. He is God, even the complete God.

B. Being a Man of Blood and Flesh Who Was Born of Blood and Flesh, Possessing the Perfect Human Nature

This Christ is the complete God according to His divine nature and the perfect man according to His human nature. He is the complete God mingled with the perfect man.

C. Being One Who Is Both God and Man— a God-man—a Mingling of the Divine Nature with the Human Nature, without a Third Nature Being Produced

D. Being the Embodiment of the Fullness of the Godhead of the Complete God

Therefore, He is One who is both God and man; He is a God-man. This God-man was a mingling of the divine nature with the human nature, without a third nature being produced. This may be likened to soaking tea leaves in water to produce tea. Neither the nature of the tea nor the nature of the water is lost. Both natures still exist and are mingled together, without a third nature being produced. Some people misunderstand us and say that concerning the God-man, we teach that the divine nature disappeared, the human nature was changed, and a third nature was produced. This is a heresy which we have never taught. This is not what we have seen from the Bible. The Lord Jesus is the mingling of two natures as one entity, without a third nature being produced. He is One who is both God and man.

I hope that you, brothers and sisters, will apply the effort to study so that you may know how the Lord Jesus as God is all-inclusive and unlimited and how He as a man is also all-inclusive and unlimited. If He was merely a man and not the God-man, then He could neither be all-inclusive nor unlimited since, as we all know, man is neither all-inclusive nor unlimited. However, because as the God-man the Lord Jesus was God mingled with man, and since God is all-inclusive and unlimited, the Lord Jesus as such a man was also all-inclusive and unlimited. This may be likened to a glass of plain water which is without any flavor, but when tea is added, the flavor gets into the water. Man is finite, but when he has God mingled with him, he becomes infinite. Man is not all-inclusive, but when he has God mingled with him, he becomes all-inclusive.

III. THE SIN-BEARING GOD-MAN
IN HIS VICARIOUS DEATH—THE REDEEMER

Finally, Christ is the Redeemer. We all know that Jesus is the Redeemer, but what we know is too general, too vague, and too superficial. We must study in depth the statuses in which He came to be our Redeemer.

A. As the One Who Is Both God and Man, Passing through Death in His Humanity with His Divinity

Who was the One who was crucified on the cross? Was He God? Some may not dare to answer this question. Can God be crucified? No one believes that man can nail God on the cross.

God cannot be crucified. Who, then, was put to death on the cross? We should say that the One who was both God and man was crucified. On the cross, He was crucified in His humanity with His divinity. Strictly speaking, He did not die there, but He passed through death. Dying is one thing, and passing through death is another thing. When we humans die, we truly die. However, instead of dying, He passed through death. Even His death was His work; He did a great deal of work at the time of His death. What work did He do? He did a saving and redeeming work. His saving and His redeeming were accomplished through His death. Human death cannot accomplish anything, but the Lord Jesus' death on the cross was His great work.

At that time the One whom the Jews arrested was not merely God but a man, yet that man had God inside of Him. Likewise, the One whom they crucified was not merely God but a man, but that man had God in Him. Therefore, the One who died on the cross was both God and man, and His death was a death in humanity with divinity. Furthermore, He did not die there, strictly speaking; rather, He passed through death. The Jews thought that when they killed Him, everything would be over. However, this was not the case with Him. On the contrary, His crucifixion offered Him the best opportunity to be exceedingly active and to do a great amount of work in His death. Therefore, He did not merely die but passed through death.

B. As a Created Man, Bearing Man's Sins and Dying for Every Created Thing

Second, He died on the cross as a created man. Since He had blood and flesh, He was truly a man, and since He was a man, He was a creature. Today some Christians oppose this truth, but Paul said that Christ is the Firstborn of all creation. He bore the sins of the world as a created man. If He were not a man, how could He have borne our sins and died for us? He tasted death on behalf of every created thing; that is, He died for everything. Since He was a created man, as such, He bore all our wrong doings, trespasses, and sinful acts and died on the cross for us. When He died there, He died on behalf of every created thing. When man sinned, he defiled every created thing. Hence, all created things needed Christ to taste death on their behalf.

C. As a Man of Flesh, Being Made Sin on Behalf of Man and Condemning Sin in the Flesh

Third, as a man who was flesh, He was made sin on behalf of man. This is so mysterious that we cannot explain it thoroughly. The Bible says clearly in 2 Corinthians 5:21 that Him who did not know sin God made sin on our behalf. God not only caused Him to bear our sins but even made Him sin on our behalf. When He was crucified on the cross, in God's eyes, sin was crucified there. When He bore our sins, He dealt with our sins, our sinful acts, but when He was made sin, He dealt with our sin, our sinful nature.

In theology, sin is divided into two categories. One category is our own sins, the sins committed by ourselves; these are our sinful acts. Another category is the original sin which came from Adam; that is our sinful nature. That is why the Lord Jesus had various statuses on the cross. As a created man He bore our sinful acts, our own sins. Furthermore, He was in the likeness of the flesh of sin, and as such a One He was made sin on our behalf. In this way He dealt with our sinful nature so that God could condemn the sinful nature which we inherited from Adam.

D. The Blood That Was Shed Being the Blood of Jesus (Humanity), the Son of God (Divinity), and Being the Blood of a Genuine Man with the Eternal and Unlimited Efficacy of God

Fourth, the blood shed by Him was the blood of Jesus, the Son of God. In the Son of God was divinity, and in Jesus was humanity. Hence, His blood was the blood of both God and man. In Acts 20:28 Paul charged the elders in Ephesus to shepherd "the church of God, which He obtained through His own blood." This verse speaks of God's own blood. Perhaps you have never thought that the blood shed by Jesus on the cross was God's own blood and that, at the same time, it was also man's blood because He was a man. For the redemption of man's sins, genuine human blood must be shed. The blood of calves and goats cannot redeem man from his sins. Only man's own blood can do this. However, because man is limited, the efficacy of man's blood is also limited. Nevertheless, the Lord Jesus was also God, and the blood He shed was the blood of the Son of God. The Son of God is infinite; hence, the efficacy of His blood is boundless and eternal. This explains why He alone could die for millions of people. If He was only a perfect man, He could die only for one person but not for millions of people. However, He was a God-man. His being a man denotes that the nature of His blood is genuine human blood, while His being God denotes that the efficacy of His blood is eternal and limitless. It is unlimited both in time and in space. Thus, His blood can wash away the sins of millions of people in all places and at all times. This is what it means to be both all-inclusive and unlimited.

E. Being the Eternal (Unlimited) Redeemer Who Accomplished an Eternal (Unlimited) Redemption

Therefore, the redemption which He accomplished by the shedding of His blood is an eternal redemption. Eternal means unlimited. He accomplished an eternal, unlimited redemption. His blood is unlimited, His redemption is unlimited, and therefore, He as the Redeemer is also unlimited. This is His all-inclusiveness, and this is also His unlimitedness.

F. Being the Divine Grain Which Passed through Death to Bring Forth Many Grains

Finally, in His death He had another status—He was the divine grain of wheat. All the previous statuses were for bearing and taking away our sins so that our sinful acts and sinful nature could be dealt with. They were for solving our problems on the negative side. Now on the positive side, He was the divine grain that fell into the ground to die to bring forth innumerable grains, including you and me. Do not forget that the grains are so many that they are truly innumerable. From the first century to His second coming, how many grains do you believe He will have? He is multiplying all the time. He is unlimited and all-inclusive. We truly have seen that our Lord is both all-inclusive and unlimited in what He is.

CHAPTER TWO

IN HIS WORK

Scripture Reading: John 1:1, 14; 1 Tim. 3:16; Luke 24:19; Acts 2:22; 10:38-39; 1 Pet. 2:24; 3:18; Heb. 2:9; Acts 13:33; 1 Pet. 1:3; 2 Pet. 1:4; 1 Cor. 15:45b; 2 Cor. 3:6b; Acts 2:36; Eph. 1:22, 10; Acts 2:33

OUTLINE

I. Being incarnated to bring God into man that divinity and humanity may be mingled as one—John 1:1, 14; 1 Tim. 3:16.

II. Passing through human living to live the human life in His humanity with His divinity—Luke 24:19; Acts 2:22; 10:38-39.

III. Dying for the creation to taste death on behalf of all creation in His humanity with His divinity—1 Pet. 2:24; 3:18; Heb. 2:9.

IV. Resurrecting from the dead:

A. To bring man into God that humanity may be mingled with divinity—Acts 13:33; 1 Pet. 1:3; 2 Pet. 1:4.

B. To become the life-giving Spirit for the dispensing of God's life into man—1 Cor. 15:45b; 2 Cor. 3:6b.

V. Ascending to the heavens:

A. To be made by God both Lord and Christ—Acts 2:36.

B. To be given by God to be Head over all things to the church that all things may be headed up in Him—Eph. 1:22, 10.

C. To pour out on His Body the all-inclusive Spirit promised by God—Acts 2:33.

In the previous message we saw that in what He is, in His person, the Lord Jesus is both all-inclusive and unlimited. A great deal is involved with His being God and His being all-inclusive and unlimited. Therefore, the Bible says that He is the mystery of God. The universe is a mystery, and God is even more a mystery, but this mystery has been unfolded in Jesus Christ. Jesus Christ is the mystery of God; outside of Him, no one can find God. Furthermore, all the fullness of the Godhead dwells in Christ bodily. How all-inclusive and boundless He is!

Even His coming to be a man was not simple. He was not a man who had only the human nature. Rather, He was a man who had the divine nature added to His human nature. His human nature was mingled with the divine nature. He was born of a human virgin, but He was conceived of the divine Holy Spirit. Therefore, He was born as a man with both the human nature and the divine nature. Thus, He could be called a God-man, One who was both God and man. When He was on the earth for thirty-three and a half years, very often even the disciples who followed Him were so amazed that they asked who this One was. He was indeed a man. He felt weary, He was hungry, He even wept and shed tears, and He slept. In this way He was the same as any normal human being. He lived as an ordinary man in a carpenter's home for thirty years. Nevertheless, many times His words and actions were extraordinary. Not only did He perform signs and wonders, but His words were simple yet great. Throughout the ages no philosopher has had the boldness to speak what He spoke. He said, "I am the life," "I am the light," and "He who follows Me shall not walk in darkness." We could not even dream of such words, which are simple yet full of wisdom. Such mysterious, excellent, and deep words indicate that He was the infinite God. Even though He was a man who was finite, in this finite man was divinity. Therefore, as a man He was both all-inclusive and infinite. Moreover, concerning His death, He did not die for Himself because He Himself did not need to die. He died for us, and He did a work for us. Even though He passed through death, He still worked in this death. The work which He carried out in His death also manifested His all-inclusiveness and unlimitedness.

FIVE CRUCIAL POINTS OF CHRIST'S WORK

In this message we want to go on and look further at how all-inclusive and unlimited He is in His work, that is, in His doings, actions, and moves. Of course, if a man is great, His actions will also be great. Since our Lord is all-inclusive and unlimited, His work surely is also all-inclusive and unlimited.

Concerning Christ, the New Testament mostly speaks of His work, which is simply His living. His living was mingled with His work. He had no office hours or off hours. He lived and He worked twenty-four hours a day. His every word and every move were His living, and His every word and every move were also His work. The Bible, especially the New Testament, uses only very simple words and brief records when referring to His person. However, the Bible speaks about His work, His move, His doings, and His words and deeds, which all constitute His living, in a rich and detailed way in chapter after chapter. From the record in these many chapters, we have extracted five crucial points concerning His actions and work: being incarnated, passing through human living, dying for the creation, resurrecting from the dead, and ascending to the heavens.

Let us now consider these five crucial points. *Being incarnated* does not sound like proper Chinese or any foreign language; this is truly the heavenly language. *Passing through human living* is somewhat ordinary, for we all must pass through human living. However, the next item, *dying for the creation,* is very extraordinary because this dying is not only for man but for everything that was created. Who can die for others? One may die for a companion out of kindness, righteousness, or love, but no one can die for the creation, that is, for the heavens, the earth, everyone, and everything. This is not only great but also all-inclusive. When a man dies, he himself dies. However, the death of Jesus Christ was an exceptional death, a death in which the heavens and the earth died with Him, all things were baptized with Him, and you and I were terminated with Him. Paul said, "I am crucified with Christ" (Gal. 2:20). Christ's crucifixion included you and me. Paul also said, "Our old man has been crucified with Him" (Rom. 6:6). When Christ died on the cross, it was not only one single Nazarene, Jesus, who died there. His death included the heavens, the earth, and everything so that you and I, we all, died together with Him. Humanly speaking, when someone dies, he is finished because to die is to be ended. The biographies of great men always conclude with their death or burial. When Jesus died, the Jews may have shouted with joy, thinking that they had eliminated Him. When they were accusing the Lord Jesus, they shouted, "Take this man away! Crucify Him!" Eventually, they achieved their purpose—they crucified Him on the cross and did away with Him. Little did they know that less than seventy-two hours later, this Jesus would walk out of death with vigorous steps. Strictly speaking, He did not go to die. He went to have a tour of the domain of death, and after He had accomplished great things in Hades, He walked out from there and resurrected. This is called His resurrection from the dead. All this was His work.

After His resurrection He stayed with the disciples for forty days to train them to experience His invisible presence. The three and a half years of His presence with the disciples was visible, which they truly enjoyed. After His crucifixion, that presence suddenly disappeared, and they became despondent to the uttermost. However, in less than seventy-two hours, He suddenly came back. In His resurrection, He was transfigured into the all-inclusive Spirit to be with them for eternity. This kind of presence, which was invisible and in spirit, was hard for the disciples to adjust to. Therefore, in those forty days, He sometimes appeared to the disciples and sometimes disappeared in front of them. In this way He trained them to experience His invisible presence.

Forty days after His resurrection, He ascended to the heavens. His ascension was also His work. On the one hand, He is resting in the heavens because He is sitting down on His throne. However, on the other hand, the Bible tells us that today in the heavens He is our High Priest, our Mediator, the King of kings, and the Lord of lords. He is the

Administrator in the universe today. If we know world history, we can see that in the past twenty centuries, from Christ's ascension up to this day, everything on this earth has been under the ruling authority of Jesus Christ. The Gregorian calendar used by the whole world today is Jesus Christ's calendar. According to world history, whosever calendar you use means you belong to that one. Today on earth, even those nations which oppose Christ use the calendar of our Lord. This proves that Jesus Christ is the real Lord. He is the King of kings and the Lord of lords. Today He sits on the throne, exercising His authority to rule over all the situations on earth that He may produce what He has desired to obtain throughout the generations, which is the Body, the church, planned by God in eternity.

Today, because of the convenience in transportation and the developments in communication, the globe seems to be much smaller. I can testify to this. Fifty-two years ago when I first began to serve the Lord, I took a boat from my hometown Chefoo in the province of Shantung to Shanghai. Such a short distance took me forty-eight hours. Since the boat was small and the waves were high, I became very sick. However, today, it takes only twelve and a half hours to come to Taiwan by airplane from Los Angeles, and it takes only one and a half days to make a round trip. It is very convenient. In addition, twenty years ago I often spent a great amount of time writing and answering letters. Sometimes I spent half a day without finishing even two or three letters. Today, however, there is no need to go to all that trouble. All I need to do is to pick up the phone. In just one phone call I can have a clear discussion of a certain matter and get an answer in five minutes. Sometimes I have called Brazil, Stuttgart, and Taipei; within an hour a certain matter related to America, Europe, and Asia was settled. People in the world claim that all these conveniences are for the advancement of civilization and the elevation of human living, but we have to say that these conveniences are for the spreading of the gospel.

Moreover, no one ever imagined that today's American English would have become a language that is commonly used throughout the whole earth. Similarly, before the Lord

Jesus was born, the Roman Empire ruled over the world surrounding the Mediterranean Sea. The Lord arranged the environment that He might be born in Bethlehem to fulfill the prophecy in Micah 5:2 in the Old Testament. At that time, Greek was commonly used within the Roman Empire, and the transportation by land or by sea could take people wherever they wanted to go. Therefore, after the Lord's death and resurrection, the disciples traveled throughout the world, and they preached the gospel wherever they went. We thank and praise the Lord that even though there are all manner of oppositions on the earth, history has proved that all the situations on the earth are for the facilitation of the preaching of the gospel. Who did this? This was done by the ascended Jesus. These five major steps—being incarnated, passing through human living, dying for the creation, resurrecting from the dead, and ascending to the heavens—are concerned with the accomplishments and the work of the Lord Jesus Christ.

In the previous message, we saw the meaning of the name *Jesus. Je-* stands for *Jehovah,* and *-sus* means *Savior.* Therefore, *Jesus* means *Jehovah the Savior.* The meaning of *Christ* in Greek is *the anointed One. Anointed* is a biblical term; the common expression is *to be commissioned, to be sent,* or *to receive a charge.* Jesus Christ is the complete God becoming a perfect man to carry out God's commission. The carrying out of His commission is His work, which is also His move.

His initial work was to create the heavens and the earth. John 1:3 says, "Apart from Him not one thing came into being which has come into being." Therefore, the first step of His work was creation. Perhaps some may ask why, since the first step of God's work is creation, I did not include this point in the outline of this message concerning His work. This is because the creation of all things was His preliminary work. Even though we regard the heavens and the earth as being very vast and all the creation as consisting of many items, they are not very important in God's economy. The creation of all things is just the preliminary work to gain a group of people, that the Triune God may work Himself into them so that they can have the same life and nature as He has. This does not mean that since we have been saved and have God's life and nature, we become God with His Godhead to be worshipped by men. This is a great heresy, and it is blasphemous and offensive to God. However, if we say that as the saved ones we have been born of God to be His children and that we possess His Spirit and His life but not His nature, this is also a wrong teaching because 2 Peter 1:4 tells us clearly that God has made us partakers of His divine nature. This is an extraordinary matter. What does it mean to be saved? To be saved is to have God come into us so that His life becomes our life, and His nature becomes our nature, because we have been born of God. If we are born of man, but we say that we do not have man's life and nature, are we not talking nonsense? We partake of the life and nature of whatever we were born of. Since our natural, physical man was born of human parents, of course, we have man's life and nature. When we were saved by believing in the Lord, we were regenerated. This is to be born not of man but of God. Since we were born of God, how can we not have God's life and nature? Hallelujah, we have God's life, and we also have God's nature! The creation of all things was not God's primary work but His preliminary work. Today God's main work is to work Himself into man.

I. BEING INCARNATED TO BRING GOD INTO MAN
THAT DIVINITY AND HUMANITY
MAY BE MINGLED AS ONE

Where then did this work begin? This work began with the Lord Jesus becoming flesh, which is called His incarnation. Therefore, incarnation was a great step in His work and a great initiation of the divine work. God entered into the womb of a human virgin and was conceived by being mingled with humanity. He stayed in the human womb for as long as nine months, and then He was born. Such a man not only possessed humanity, but in His humanity there was also divinity.

Brothers and sisters, we need to see that the Lord's incarnation was truly a great matter. It was much greater than the creation of the heavens and the earth. In the creation of the heavens and the earth, "He spoke, and it was; / He commanded, and it stood" (Psa. 33:9). When God said, "Let there be light," light came. However, it was not as simple for God to work Himself into man. He Himself had to go into a human womb and stay there for nine months. To speak and command things into being can only be used in the creation of the heavens and the earth; it cannot be used in the matter of God working Himself into man. This required the complete God to enter personally into a human womb to stay there for nine months and then be born. What a pity that today, when people celebrate Christmas, not merely the unbelievers but even those in Christianity, they are too superficial! They do not enter into the depths to see the mystery of God's incarnation.

Brothers and sisters, I hope that all of us can see that the first major step in this divine, great, eternal, all-inclusive, and unlimited work was God's incarnation. The incarnation of God was the entering of God into man, divinity being mingled with humanity. Soon after Adam was created, he fell and missed the goal of God. God's goal was for him as a vessel to contain God, signified by the tree of life. However, Adam was tempted, he ate of the wrong tree, and he was poisoned. When God came to the garden, both Adam and Eve were so frightened that they hid themselves; they were afraid to see God. Thank God that He still had the grace of redemption! He gave Eve a promise that the seed of woman would bruise the serpent's head, although the serpent would also bruise the heel of the seed of woman. We all know that this was fulfilled in the Lord Jesus. He was the seed born of a woman, and He bruised Satan's head on the cross. Thus, His first step was to advance with a great stride to enter into the womb of a virgin in a humble way, to stay there for nine months, and to be born a God-man, who was Jesus Christ, Jehovah the Savior, for the accomplishment of God's commission.

II. PASSING THROUGH HUMAN LIVING TO LIVE THE HUMAN LIFE IN HIS HUMANITY WITH HIS DIVINITY

After His birth, He lived in a poor carpenter's home. Even at the time when He went out for His work, people asked, "Is not this the carpenter?" or, "Is not this the carpenter's son?" (Mark 6:3; Matt. 13:55). Dear brothers and sisters, I am afraid that it may never have occurred to you that our God, our Savior, spent nine months in the womb of a virgin and lived in the house of a poor carpenter, not thirty days nor thirty months, but thirty years. This is something very mysterious that is hard for us to comprehend. Where was God in those thirty years? Was He in the tall and great temple in Jerusalem, or was He in the house of that carpenter in Nazareth? For all those thirty years God was in the house of that poor carpenter in Nazareth. Therefore, in those thirty years those who wanted to worship God had to go to the house of that poor carpenter in Nazareth and not to the temple in Jerusalem. In the house of that poor carpenter the Lord Jesus passed through human living a small step at a time. When the thirty years were fulfilled, He went out to preach. Before He began His ministry He was baptized, indicating to the universe that He forsook Himself and lived absolutely by God. When He came out of the water, the heavens opened, and the Holy Spirit descended like a dove upon Him. In studying the Bible we have a problem here. Since the Lord Jesus was conceived of the Holy Spirit, did He not have the Holy Spirit already within Him? Why was it that at the time of His baptism the Holy Spirit came again from the heavens? Were there two Holy Spirits? When I was young, I did not understand this matter. Gradually, after I gained some experience in my study of the Bible and through the use of Bible expositions written throughout the centuries, I finally understood that the Holy Spirit of whom Jesus was conceived was the essential Spirit for His living, and the Holy Spirit who descended upon Jesus after His baptism was the economical Spirit for His work.

What the lowly Jesus did on the earth was to carry out God's economy. What then is God's economy? The economy of God is to redeem His created yet fallen men back to their original situation, and then to put Himself into them, His redeemed ones. Through His death and the shedding of His blood on the cross, He redeemed fallen men. After this work was done, He resurrected, and in His resurrection He became

the life-giving Spirit. When we call on the name of the Lord
Jesus, this life-giving Spirit comes into us. This is God
coming into us. The Lord Jesus came to the earth to accomplish this very thing. In the first thirty years, He lived in a
carpenter's house. In the last three and a half years, He went
out to do the work of preaching. He cast out demons, healed
the sick, performed miracles, prophesied, and spoke words of
wisdom, testifying that He was the all-inclusive and unlimited God. One day, He was in a home in Bethany where there
was a love feast. People loved Him, and one poured ointment
on His head. I would ask again, when He was attending that
love feast and was being anointed in that home in Bethany,
would you say that God was in that small house in Bethany
or in the holy temple in Jerusalem? Now we are clear, and we
have the boldness to say that God was in Bethany and not in
Jerusalem. He was in that small house and not in the holy
temple. In the holy temple, the priests considered God as the
One who was high above them and who could only be revered
but could not be approached. Yet, in the small house of Bethany, not only was God revered, but He was also approachable
and lovable. He was so approachable that John could recline
on His bosom. We thank and praise the Lord that sinners can
be saved to such an extent as to enter into God's embrace.

III. DYING FOR THE CREATION TO TASTE DEATH
ON BEHALF OF ALL CREATION
IN HIS HUMANITY WITH HIS DIVINITY

Not only so, but once He passed through human living, He
went one great step further to die for the creation. Apparently,
the Lord was crucified because He was betrayed by Judas,
arrested by the servants of the high priest, and condemned to
death by Pilate. Actually, it was He Himself who helped to
materialize His crucifixion. If you study the Bible carefully,
you can see that when the Lord Jesus was in Galilee, He went
hurriedly to Jerusalem because the Passover was approaching. Why did He do this? It was because that year was the time
for the completion of the sixty-ninth week of the seventy
weeks mentioned in Daniel 9:24-26. It was very clearly mentioned there that during the sixty-ninth week, the Messiah,

who was Christ, would be cut off, that is, killed. He knew that at the Passover of that year, He would be crucified. He also knew that He had to die in Jerusalem on Mount Moriah, where Abraham had offered Isaac and which was later called Mount Zion. Furthermore, according to the type of the Passover, He had to die on the fourteenth day of the first month. Therefore, He went quickly from Galilee to Jerusalem.

Six days before the Passover, He entered Jerusalem, giving the Jews four days to examine Him. This was also for the fulfillment of the type in the Bible. According to Exodus 12:3-6, the Passover lamb, which was to be without blemish, had to be prepared in the four days preceding the Passover. Therefore, in those four days, He placed Himself in the temple under the meticulous examination of the Sadducees, Pharisees, chief priests, scribes, and elders. After examining Him for four days, they found no fault in Him. Then they arrested Him and delivered Him up to be examined by a Gentile official. Yet, Pilate said three times, "I find no fault in this man." He was truly the sinless Lamb, the Lamb without any defects or blemishes. Hence, He was worthy to die on our behalf. By this we can see that in actuality He was not arrested by men; rather, He delivered Himself up. He walked into death Himself. However, He did not go merely to die; instead, He passed through death to do His work. A certain portion of His work had to be done in death. If He did not enter into death, He could not have done that work. He went into death to accomplish a great work.

As we have pointed out in the past, the Lord Jesus died on the cross in seven statuses. First, He was the Lamb of God; second, He was a man in the flesh; third, He was the One signified by the bronze serpent; fourth, He was the last Adam; fifth, He was the Firstborn of all creation; sixth, He was the Peacemaker and the peace; and seventh, He was also a grain of wheat. When He died on the cross, He died in these seven statuses.

In other words, His death included at least seven aspects. First, He was the Lamb of God who took away the sin of the world. Second, He was a man in the flesh who was considered sin by God; He did not know sin but was made sin by God, and in His flesh God condemned our sinful nature. Third, He was the bronze serpent with the serpent's form but without the serpent's poison. As such, when He was judged on the cross, He destroyed Satan, the ancient serpent. Fourth, He was the last Adam, the last old man. Therefore, when He died, He crucified the old man and ended the human race. Thus, Romans 6:6 says that our old man has been crucified with Him. Fifth, He was the Firstborn of all creation, and He died as a creature, representing all the creation. This may be compared to the veil in the temple in the Old Testament. The veil signified His flesh, and on the veil were embroidered cherubim, the four living creatures. When the veil was rent, the four living creatures were also rent. This meant that when Christ died, all the creation died and was terminated with Him. Sixth, when He died on the cross, He abolished all the ordinances. The Judaic ordinances made it impossible for the Jews to be one with the Gentiles. Every people has its own ordinances, and every place has its own customs and habits. All these resulted in dividing the peoples on the earth into nations. He abolished all these ordinances on the cross.

Lastly, He died on the cross as a grain of wheat sown into the ground. On the positive side, He released the divine life that was within Him to produce many grains, which are the tens of millions who believe in Him. All these grains are made into one bread, which is one Body, the church. How all-inclusive and unlimited His death is! Why is it unlimited? It is because He was crucified in His humanity with His divinity. We can illustrate this by a grain of wheat sown into the soil. On the one hand, the grain dies because its shell decays. At the same time, however, the life within the grain begins to operate and grow. Therefore, 1 Peter 3:18 says that when Christ was on the cross, He was put to death in the flesh but made alive in the Spirit. This is just like the grain of wheat. According to its outer shell, it is decaying, but according to its inner life, it operates to bring forth tender sprouts. This is a picture of resurrection.

IV. RESURRECTING FROM THE DEAD

In God's eyes, when Christ was resurrected, not only He alone was resurrected, but all of us who have been chosen and counted by God to be in Christ were also resurrected together with Him. Just as in His death He brought all of us with Him to pass through death, so also in His resurrection from the dead He brought us out of death into resurrection. Therefore, Ephesians 2:6 says that God raised us up together with Christ and seated us together with Him in the heavenlies. First Peter 1:3 also tells us that God regenerated us through the resurrection of Christ. Never think that you were not regenerated until you believed in the Lord. This manner of accounting is wrong. You were regenerated on the same day as Peter and John, which was the day of the Lord's resurrection. The day in which the Lord Jesus was resurrected was also the day in which you were regenerated. God is eternal; with Him there is no factor of time or space. In His eyes, all the saved ones were regenerated with Christ on the same day.

God chose us before the foundation of the world. At that time, not only were we not yet born, but even the angels, the heavens, and the earth were not yet created. In the eyes of God, however, we already existed at that time. Brothers and sisters, do you believe that you already existed before the foundation of the world? Ephesians 1:4-5 says that God chose us and predestinated us. Predestination is a marking out. If we had not existed in eternity, how could God have chosen and predestinated us? We cannot comprehend this in our mind. However, to God, you and I existed long, long ago in this universe, and God chose and predestinated us at that time. One day, He came to die for us, and after everything was accomplished, He was also resurrected for us. Then at a certain time we were born and grew up, and somehow we heard the gospel and believed in Jesus. Previously, the gospel may have seemed like a superstition to us, but we could not help believing it. Moreover, the more we believed, the more comfortable and happy we were. Have you seen a family or nation that believes in Jesus but is not blessed?

Dear brothers and sisters, we truly must understand that we are those chosen by God and that when the Lord Jesus was crucified, He also brought us to the cross. He is all-inclusive, His death is all-inclusive, and His resurrection is limitless. When a grain of wheat dies, many grains are produced. What is sown is one grain, but what is brought forth are many grains. One Jesus was buried in the tomb, but tens of millions of people were resurrected. Today we are all in Christ. Very often we feel weak in ourselves, and we all have many problems. However, the Lord's word tells us that in Christ we can do all things. In Christ, we are all strong and not weak. Do not believe in your weakness; that is Satan's lie. Each one of us is strong because we are the resurrected ones, and today we are sitting in the heavenlies.

A. To Bring Man into God
That Humanity May Be Mingled with Divinity

Christ resurrected from the dead to bring man into God that humanity may be mingled with divinity.

B. To Become the Life-giving Spirit
for the Dispensing of God's Life into Man

Christ also resurrected from the dead to become the life-giving Spirit for the dispensing of God's life into man.

V. ASCENDING TO THE HEAVENS

A. To Be Made by God Both Lord and Christ

Dear brothers and sisters, there are no words which are more excellent and trustworthy than the words of the Bible. The Bible tells us that we have been chosen by God and that God has put us in Christ. When Christ died, we died together with Him. When Christ resurrected, we were raised up together with Him. When Christ ascended, we ascended with Him to the heavenlies and were seated with Him on the throne. Today, we look neither at the environment nor at our own condition. We look only at Him. As the Lord in the heavens today, this Jesus rules over everything, and as Christ, He accomplishes everything.

B. To Be Given by God to Be Head
over All Things to the Church
That All Things May Be Headed Up in Him

He is also the Head over all things for the church and to

the church, so that all things may be headed up in Him. The people of the world are sinful and degraded. Sin and degradation cause people to be scattered. However, when we believe in the Lord Jesus, He heads us up in Himself. Therefore, today when we preach the gospel, we bring people into the Lord Jesus. All those people who believe will be headed up in Christ as the Head.

C. To Pour Out on His Body the All-inclusive Spirit Promised by God

Lastly, when He ascended to the heavens and received the all-inclusive Spirit from the Father, He poured this Spirit out upon all who believe in Him. In this Spirit we have become one Body, which is the church. When I come to this point, my heart is so joyful and my spirit leaps. Glory, hallelujah! We who are in Christ have been seated together with Him in the heavenlies, and we have the Holy Spirit poured out upon us to make us one Body for His testimony.

CHAPTER THREE

IN HIS MULTIPLICATION AND INCREASE

Scripture Reading: John 12:24; Luke 12:50; Rom. 8:3; Eph.
2:15; 1 Pet. 3:18; 1:3; 1 Cor. 12:12, 27; 10:17; John 3:30

OUTLINE

I. As the divine grain of wheat (John 12:24) He being
constrained in the shell of His flesh—Luke 12:50.

II. Through His all-inclusive death He dying in His
fleshly shell—Rom. 8:3; Eph. 2:15.

III. While He was dying in His fleshly shell, He grow-
ing in His divine life and entering into resurrection—
1 Pet. 3:18.

IV. In His resurrection His divine life bearing fruit and
multiplying into countless grains—1 Pet. 1:3; John
12:24.

V. These countless grains being His many members
which constitute His eternal, mystical Body—1 Cor.
12:12, 27; 10:17.

VI. This mystical Body being His eternal, boundless
increase—John 3:30.

This message is high, deep, and mysterious. We may say that this is the highest, deepest, and most mysterious truth in the Bible. Therefore, we need to calm down our entire being and allow the Lord to operate in every way in our spirit that we may be enlightened in our understanding and may have a sober mind to enter into this profound truth.

A HISTORY OF THE UNLOCKING
OF THE BIBLICAL TRUTHS

The Bible was completed at the end of the first century when the writing of Revelation was finished. However, up to now, the believers' exposition and knowledge of the Bible have not reached the final point. Of course, as early as the second century, some great Bible expositors, who in church history are called the church fathers, had already interpreted a great deal concerning the Bible. From that time until now, in every age there have been many who have studied and learned the biblical truths. History shows us that this study or learning is not individual but corporate, involving all the believers, and it is also progressive, becoming clearer century by century. Of course, from A.D. 570, after the papal system had fully become established, the Bible was locked up for ten centuries. That period of time is referred to in history as the Dark Ages. For one thousand years, human society was in darkness because the Bible had been sealed.

Thereafter, Martin Luther and some of his contemporaries rose up to bring in the Reformation, and risking their lives, they opened the closed Bible. Moreover, printing was invented at that time, so the spreading of the Bible no longer depended on copying by hand but on printing. Thus the Bible was released from its imprisonment and could be distributed in large quantities. However, at that time the contents of the Bible were not very open, and people's understanding of the Bible was very limited. Thus the Bible seemed to remain a sealed book.

From the Reformation in the time of Martin Luther, throughout the centuries one Bible expositor after another was raised up to unravel some of the biblical truths. However, the degree of the unraveling was very limited. This situation lasted for about four centuries, beginning from the time of Luther, through the time of Zinzendorf, and proceeding to the previous century, the nineteenth century. In the 1820s, the Lord raised up the Brethren in England. Once they were raised up, the light of the truths flooded like a waterfall. From that time onward, the Bible was formally opened to us. We thank and praise the Lord for this!

TWO DIFFERENT THEOLOGICAL TEACHINGS OF RECENT TIMES

In recent times, the study of biblical truths, the so-called theology, has produced different kinds of teachings. One theology, which became accepted after the Reformation, was nearly heretical. It acknowledged the Bible, it acknowledged God, and it also acknowledged that the Lord Jesus was the Son of God who became a man, that He died on the cross for sinners, that He was resurrected from the dead, and that He ascended to heaven. However, concerning His second coming, its teaching was incorrect. This school of theology taught that human society will gradually improve due to the influence of the gospel and the teaching of the truth, and that one day, a "utopia" will appear, which will be the millennial kingdom. However, the Bible tells us clearly that human society has no way to improve itself. On the contrary, it will become more and more evil until its sins overflow. Then at the end of this age, the Lord Jesus will come back to judge the people in the world and rule as King on the earth. Furthermore, He will change the world situation into the heavenly kingdom for a thousand years. Therefore, the teaching of this school of theology is far off from the biblical truths.

Before the First World War in Europe, at the beginning of the 1900s, this type of theology was very popular. Especially in Europe, many people believed that European society would gradually improve through the spread of the gospel and the teaching of the truth. Contrary to their belief, in 1914 the war broke out in Europe, and it developed to such an extent that the whole world was engaged in the conflict. Consequently, their teaching concerning the transformation of their society into the heavenly kingdom evaporated. That was why in 1918, at the end of the First World War, people put this kind of teaching aside and came back to study the prophecies in the Bible.

At that time, the publications put out by Christianity were mostly expositions of biblical prophecies. I was saved at precisely that time, and of all the reference books I obtained, most of them were to help in the understanding of the prophecies in the Bible. I can testify that many of the prophecies that I read or studied over fifty years ago have been fulfilled in these fifty or more years. For example, at that time I read that the nation of Israel would be restored and that the Jews would recover Jerusalem. When I read this, I did not dare to disbelieve because that was the word of the Bible. However, I shook my head, saying in my heart, "How can there be such a thing?" The Jews had lost their country for nearly two thousand years. Their territory was absolutely gone and their people were scattered among all the other peoples all over the world. How could they ever become a nation again? This seemed impossible. For Jerusalem to be returned to the Jews also seemed impossible. The Crusades were launched because the Arabs, who were Moslems, took possession of the holy city, Jerusalem. That was the reason the Christians in Europe formed armies of Crusaders to make a number of eastern conquests to recapture Jerusalem. Eventually, however, they did not succeed, and the holy city still remained in the hands of the Moslems. The Moslems built a mosque on Mount Zion in Jerusalem at the old site of the holy temple. That is the second largest mosque, which is smaller only than the mosque in Mecca. However in 1948 after the Second World War, suddenly the Jews reestablished their nation. Furthermore, the nation of Israel was immediately recognized by the United Nations. Then after nineteen years, in 1967, Jerusalem was returned to the Jews. That was truly a miracle. The biblical prophecies which I read fifty to sixty years ago have mostly been fulfilled.

The First World War ended in 1918, and from the viewpoint of Europe, only twenty-one years elapsed before Hitler started the war again in 1939. Actually, before that, in 1931 when Japan invaded the headquarters in Feng-tien, which was in

Manchuria, China, that was the beginning of World War II. Counting from that day, there were only thirteen years from the end of one war to the beginning of another. In World War II, the whole world was engaged in the conflict, so much so that everything was in disarray. As a result, the erroneous theology of the millennial kingdom was completely destroyed, and no one would believe in it any longer. One of the main errors of this kind of theology was the belief that human nature can be changed and that Christians do not receive another nature, a spiritual nature, through regeneration. We acknowledge that every saved person has two natures. One comes from his birth and the other from regeneration. Nevertheless, this theology did not acknowledge this. I am speaking only this much to you so you may realize that whenever you hear the word *theology,* it does not always mean that it is something good. Actually, certain theologies, one of which is the theology of which we have spoken, contain grave errors.

Among the different theologies, the highest and most trustworthy is the Brethren theology. This type of theology rose up gradually after 1830 through the teachings of Darby and others. Today the topmost Bible seminaries in America all receive the Brethren theology, which is the most reliable. I do hope that the Bible seminaries in the Far East, both in Hong Kong and in Taiwan, will receive the Brethren theology instead of taking the way of the erroneous theology of which we have spoken. I speak these matters to you in order to show you the progression of man's knowledge of the Bible over the last two thousand years.

In recent times, Christianity, in particular Protestantism, was brought to China by Robert Morrison in the previous century, in 1807. Since that time many Western missionaries came to China, and they started to translate the Bible into Chinese. Today the Mandarin Union Version that we have in our hands is one of the best translations in the world. Its language is plain and easy to understand, its style is appropriate, and its rhythm is also very nice. Yet it is regrettable that the Western missionaries did not bring with them much knowledge of the Bible. They did not properly bring the Brethren theology to China.

The Lord raised up His recovery in China in 1922. Once we were raised up by the Lord, the thing to which we paid the most attention was the knowledge of the Bible. I can never forget how I began to write to Brother Watchman Nee soon after I was saved in 1925. My questions to him were mostly spiritual ones. Once I asked him, "Please tell me what book there is that can help me more than any other in the world to understand the Bible. I truly want to understand the Bible." He replied to my letter by saying that according to his knowledge, *The Synopsis of the Books of the Bible* by John Nelson Darby was the best in helping people to understand the Bible. He further said that because the English grammar of this book was very difficult, one could not understand it without reading it four or five times. As far back as fifty-nine years ago, when we, who were two young brothers, wrote to each other, we were trying to find out how to obtain a book that could help us the most in understanding the Bible. I remember in that same year, a certain pastor in Nanking named Cheng Chi-kwei translated the most widely circulated Scofield Bible Correspondence Course into Chinese. Brother Nee also helped in that translation, and he held it in considerable esteem. I was only at the tender age of twenty at that time, and I immediately enrolled in that course. I received considerable help by taking the course. Scofield's correspondence course and his Reference Bible are the most widely circulated in America, and over ninety percent of the truths contained in them are based on the Brethren theology.

NEW TERMS IN THE LORD'S RECOVERY

If you investigate, you will see that much of the terminology which we use today is definitely not found in Christian theology. Some among us have studied theology, and perhaps some even were pastors. I would ask them if expressions such as "the increase of Christ" and "the multiplication of Christ" have ever been used in Chinese theology. These terms were not found in theology before we were raised up by the Lord. We can say that they, especially the terms *increase* and *multiplication,* were invented by us.

Hymns, #203 was written by me in English after I brought the Lord's recovery to America, when I was preparing the English hymnal in 1963. In 1967, when I returned to Taiwan to rearrange the Chinese hymns, I translated this hymn into Chinese myself. This hymn reads as follows:

1 In the bosom of the Father,
  Ere the ages had begun,
 Thou wast in the Father's glory,
  God's unique begotten Son.
 When to us the Father gave Thee,
  Thou in person wast the same,
 All the fulness of the Father
  In the Spirit to proclaim.

2 By Thy death and resurrection,
  Thou wast made God's firstborn Son;
 By Thy life to us imparting,
  Was Thy duplication done.
 We, in Thee regenerated,
  Many sons to God became;
 Truly as Thy many brethren,
  We are as Thyself the same.

3 Once Thou wast the only grain, Lord,
  Falling to the earth to die,
 That thru death and resurrection
  Thou in life may multiply.
 We were brought forth in Thy nature
  And the many grains became;
 As one loaf we all are blended,
  All Thy fulness to proclaim.

4 We're Thy total reproduction,
  Thy dear Body and Thy Bride,
 Thine expression and Thy fulness,
  For Thee ever to abide.
 We are Thy continuation,
  Thy life-increase and Thy spread,
 Thy full growth and Thy rich surplus,
  One with Thee, our glorious Head.

In this hymn we use expressions such as *duplication, reproduction, continuation, increase, spread,* and *surplus.* These were terms which I created while I was speaking and preaching the truth. They were already in the Chinese language, but it was I who first used them in theology.

CHRIST'S INCREASE AND MULTIPLICATION

In John 3:30 John the Baptist said, "He must increase, but I must decrease." This word was not translated accurately in the Chinese version. Its translation reads, "He must prosper, but I must languish." To prosper does not necessarily mean to increase, and to languish does not necessarily mean to decrease. In the English King James Version this verse was translated quite well. It says, "He must increase, but I must decrease." It is not a matter of prospering but a matter of increasing, and it is not a matter of languishing but a matter of decreasing.

When John the Baptist went out to preach and baptize people, a considerable number of people followed him, and he introduced the Lord Jesus to them. Later, when the Lord Jesus began His ministry, quite a number of John's followers turned to follow the Lord instead. At a certain point, the Lord was baptizing even more people than John. Seeing the situation, John's disciples were not at all happy, so they came to their teacher and said, "Rabbi, He who was with you across the Jordan, of whom you have testified, behold, He is baptizing and all are coming to Him" (v. 26). Then John told them, in effect, "I have already told you that I am not the Christ. He who has the bride is the bridegroom; I am only the friend of the bridegroom. I stand by the side of the bridegroom and rejoice when I hear his voice." Therefore, he concluded by saying, "He must increase, but I must decrease."

The subject of John 3 is regeneration. From our human point of view, regeneration is for us to be saved that we may become a new man. However, from God's point of view, regeneration is for the increase of Christ. Before your regeneration, the increase of Christ was at least a fraction too small. Both you and I are very small, but even when a small one is saved, he can add a tiny bit to the increase of Christ. When the Lord

Jesus was walking on earth, at that time there was only one
Jesus on the earth. When the Lord called His disciples, some
of them, at least twelve, followed Him at His side every day.
At that time, Peter, James, and John were very near to Him,
yet they did not have Jesus within them. Jesus was in their
midst, but He was not within them. That was why there was
only one Jesus in the whole universe. However, after the Lord
Jesus died on the cross, was buried, and resurrected, He came
in the midst of the disciples in the evening of the day of His
resurrection and breathed into them, saying, "Receive the
Holy Spirit" (John 20:22). Who is the Holy Spirit? The Holy
Spirit is God Himself, the Triune God reaching man. To
breathe the Holy Spirit into man is to breathe God into man.
Therefore, in the evening of the day of His resurrection,
Christ was increased. Before that time He had been only one
Nazarene, but after that He was in a dozen or more
Galileans.

When the time of His death was approaching, it is as if the
Lord Jesus said, "Everybody welcomes Me, but I have to go
and die. I am a grain of wheat. Unless the grain of wheat falls
into the ground and dies, it abides alone; but if it dies, it bears
much fruit, at least thirtyfold, perhaps sixtyfold, or even a
hundredfold." This word of the Lord tells us that once He
passed through death and grew out of it, He would multiply
in resurrection. In this multiplication, one grain would
become many grains. This is multiplication, and this is
increase. In the beginning of Acts, in chapter one, one
hundred twenty people were there, and each one of them was
like Jesus the Nazarene. At that time there was not only one
Jesus the Nazarene but one hundred twenty-one. Then on the
day of Pentecost, when the economical Spirit descended, three
thousand people were saved. Therefore, at that time, Jesus
was three thousand one hundred twenty-onefold.

I say again, in John 12, there was only one grain—
Jesus. He was the only one. If someone has only one grain of
wheat in his barn, he is pitifully poor. However, at the time
of John 20, this grain increased because He breathed the
Spirit into those Galileans. Therefore, when we come to
Acts 1, this grain becomes one hundred twenty-one grains.

Ten days later, on the day of Pentecost, the Holy Spirit came, and three thousand were saved and baptized. Then, there were three thousand one hundred twenty-one grains. Not only so, but in Acts 4, five thousand were added, so at that time there were eight thousand one hundred twenty-one grains. Furthermore, in Acts 21 when Paul went to Jerusalem for the last time, James told him that there were tens of thousands of Jews who had received the Lord. Thus, at that time in Jerusalem there were tens of thousands of grains. That was only in one city, Jerusalem. Consider the situation today. The grains are all over the world. This is multiplication and increase. Over one hundred years ago this increase came to China, and today it has come into you. Hallelujah, Christ's multiplication has come into you! In this conference there are about seven to eight thousand who are His multiplication. On this whole earth His multiplication is countless.

Forgive me for saying that today's Christians do not see this truth of multiplication and increase when they read the Bible. Not only so, even those Christians who are teachers do not speak about this aspect. No one talks about how Christ has propagated Himself into us who believe in Him. This is a regrettable situation.

NOT RELIGION BUT THE LIVING CHRIST

Because no one speaks about this, most of today's Christians consider the Bible—the divine revelation—as a religious classic. They look on the Christian truths as a religion which teaches people according to a set of beliefs. Because of some knowledge of God and reverence for God, they worship Him, and since they worship God, they teach people according to this One whom they worship. They may say, "As a wife who fears God, you must behave properly by submitting to your husband that you may glorify God. As a husband who worships God, you also must love your wife with all gentleness that you may glorify God." We cannot say that this kind of teaching is unscriptural. However, we must realize that this kind of moral and ethical teaching is religion, in which people are taught according to whom they worship. Strictly speaking, this violates God's spiritual principle.

What is God's spiritual principle? Paul said in Galatians 2:20, "I am crucified with Christ," that is, only when I am finished can Christ propagate Himself into me. Remember that Paul spoke this word to a group of Christians who had been under Judaism. This group of religionists who were fervent for Judaism, on the one hand, received the Lord Jesus, and on the other hand, brought the practice of law-keeping into the midst of the Christians, so that they became a people with two religions. They were a people who were, on the one hand, Christians, and on the other hand, Judaizers. Paul was originally a Judaizer, but when the Lord met him on the way to Damascus, he turned fully from the Jewish religion to Christ, not to Christianity. That was why he declared boldly that he had died to the law. How did he die? He did not die by committing suicide. Rather, he was brought to the cross by Christ to die with Him in His crucifixion. "I am crucified with Christ; and it is no longer I who live, but it is Christ who lives in me" (Gal. 2:20). Who is this Jesus who lives in us? He is the Spirit who was breathed into the disciples in John 20. This Spirit is the Christ who lived in Paul. This is not Christianity but Christ. This is not religion but the living Christ. This is not to teach according to a set of beliefs. Rather, this is to pass through the death of the cross and allow Christ to multiply and increase in us.

Because to us to live is Christ, our love is far more transcendent than the love of a husband who loves his wife by himself. Because to us to live is Christ, our submission is much more spontaneous than the submission of a wife who submits to her husband by clenching her teeth. Since our submission is not merely a human submission but a submission that is lived out by the Holy Spirit and Christ in us, it is transcendent and spontaneous. Hallelujah, this is the multiplication and increase of Christ!

If as a wife you abide by religious doctrines, trying cautiously and fearfully to be a good wife every day by submitting to your husband, or if as a husband you restrain yourself with fear and trembling to be a good husband, this is not Christ's multiplication or His increase. At most, Christ has gained you as a disciple or an apprentice whom He can teach to follow Him. He has not entered into you to make you His multiplication and increase. Even though you love your wife to the uttermost, you cannot say, "I am crucified with Christ; and it is no longer I who live." On the contrary, you can boast by saying, "It is I who live." You cannot say, "It is no longer I"; rather, you can say, "Much more it is I." However, if you say, "Much more it is I," this is a shame. In God's economy, He does not care for you or me to be this or that. He only cares for Christ's multiplication and increase.

 Brothers and sisters, if the truth which we preach is different from what is preached in Christianity, the difference lies in the multiplication and increase of Christ. What a pity that today in many church buildings you cannot hear such teachings concerning the multiplication and increase of Christ, and you cannot find such textbooks in the Bible seminaries. Nevertheless, we harbor a hope that the truths which we have seen in these years will be spread among Christians in a short time. At this point, we have labored for eleven years to have two trainings every year, one in the summer and one in the winter, to specifically study the twenty-seven books in the New Testament. We have already finished twenty-six books. Recently, we published a set of nine volumes of life-studies on the exposition of Paul's fourteen Epistles. We hope that these truths can be spread to every part of the world. We have already started to do this in America. In America, there are several dozen churches. We encourage each church to contact their local libraries, especially the libraries of the Bible seminaries, and donate a set to them. Now at least a few dozen sets have been given away. Those libraries generally welcome receiving this set of life-studies. We do this in the hope that these truths will spread everywhere and reach everywhere that all may be blessed in the same way.

THE WORKS WHICH THE LORD ACCOMPLISHED IN HIS PROCESSES

We have to see that our Lord is not the founder of a religion but One who died and resurrected. From the time of His incarnation to the time of His ascension, He did a number of great works. We have already pointed out in the second chapter that the Lord's all-inclusiveness and unlimitedness are manifested in His work. Due to limitations, I was not detailed enough, so I would like to add a further word. Our Lord was incarnated, passed through human living, passed through death, entered into resurrection, and ascended to the heavens. What commission did His work fulfill? The first step He took was to bring God from heaven into man. Before Him, in the four thousand years of human history, no one had ever had God in him. Whether sages or sinners, whether good or evil, they were all alike in that they did not have God in them. Then one day, in the city of David, a child was born who was laid in a manger, and within this child was God. The Lord Jesus' incarnation brought the complete Triune God—the Father, the Son, and the Spirit—into man. That day, on the earth there was a descendent of Adam, who was Jesus the Nazarene, who had God in Him. The complete God was brought into man. Therefore, while Jesus was on the earth in those thirty-three and a half years, He became an exceedingly mysterious person. He was a genuine man, yet it was God who lived in Him. This is very mysterious.

Then when He went to the cross, He brought the created man, whom He had become, with all the creation, the devil, and sin to be crucified there. Like a huge broom, the cross gave the whole universe an extensive sweeping and thus ended the entire old creation. Satan was terminated, the demons were annihilated, sin was cleared up, and you and I were also ended there. Hallelujah, this is the cross!

As I have said before, when the Lord Jesus died, He passed through death, and while He was passing through death, He did a great work. He died in seven statuses—as the Lamb of God, the bronze serpent, the last Adam, the Firstborn of all creation, a man in the flesh, the Peacemaker, and the divine grain of wheat. He passed through death in many statuses, and in the process, He accomplished a particular work in each status. As the Lamb of God, He took away our sins. As the bronze serpent, He dealt with our sinful nature. As the last Adam, He terminated our old man. As the Firstborn of all creation, He ended all the old creation. As a man in the likeness of the flesh, He condemned sin in the flesh. As the

Peacemaker, He abolished the law of the ordinances. Furthermore, as the grain of wheat, He released the divine life. If He had not died, the divine life could not have been released. Once He died, the divine life was released from the shell of the grain of wheat. His death was truly a great step in His work. He accomplished a great work in His passing through death.

In the accomplishment of His great work, He also rested. While He was resting, He went in His living Spirit to the place where the fallen angelic spirits are imprisoned temporarily to proclaim to them. Therefore, 1 Peter 3:18 says that Christ, on the one hand, was put to death in the flesh, but on the other hand, was made alive in the Spirit. This is just like a grain of wheat that is sown into the earth. According to the outward shell, it decays and dies, but according to the life within, its organic function is activated and made alive so that it grows. Therefore, when the Lord Jesus passed through death and accomplished His work, He was strengthened, made alive, in His living Spirit, and then He walked out of death. That was His resurrection.

In such a resurrection He brought man into God. In His incarnation God was brought into man, while in His resurrection man was brought into God. We must thank and praise the Lord and shout with joy! Today there is a man sitting on the throne in the heavens. When Stephen was stoned to death, he saw the heavens opened up and the Son of Man standing at the right hand of God. Today some theologians do not believe that the Lord Jesus is still a man after His resurrection. They say that the Lord Jesus was a man only from His birth to His crucifixion, and that after His resurrection from the dead, He ceased to be a man. When He was born, He put on humanity, but once He resurrected, He put off everything of humanity. They say, therefore, that today He is not man but only God. This is a heresy. The Bible tells us clearly that today in the heavens He still has His humanity. Before His incarnation, our Lord was God, not man. From the time He put on flesh and was born on the earth, He was not only God but also man. After His resurrection and ascension, He was still not only God but also man. Nevertheless, before His resurrection, His humanity was of the old creation. After His resurrection, His humanity of the old creation was uplifted into the new creation. This may be likened to a grain of wheat, which is small and brownish in its outward form. When it is sown into the earth, its shell decays, and the germ within breaks forth. In this way the grain changes in its outward form and becomes a green sprout. The sprout grows into a stalk, and after more growth, green leaves come out. After still more growth, ears of wheat appear. Thus, after the ears are produced, its form and shape have changed.

First Corinthians 15 shows us that after the Lord Jesus resurrected from the dead, He was still a man, yet His body was a resurrected body. In the evening of the day of His resurrection, He came to the place where His disciples were and stood in their midst, although the doors were shut. The disciples thought that they saw a spirit. The Lord showed them the marks of the nails on His hands and the mark on His side to prove that He had a body. How can we explain that the resurrected Christ still has a body? I do not know how to explain this. There are many great things in this universe that we cannot explain. Our Lord resurrected, and as the Spirit He still has a resurrected body. To this day He is still a man on the throne. Praise Him!

WE BEING THE MEMBERS OF CHRIST CONSTITUTING HIS BODY AS HIS INCREASE

We must remember what kind of people we are. We have God who came into us through regeneration. Not only so, we have also entered into God in resurrection. This is a glorious fact. When we believed in the Lord Jesus and called upon His name, we received the Lord Jesus into us. We can testify that before we believed in the Lord and called upon His name, we were empty within. However, once we believe in the Lord, there is something within us that burns, shines, rebukes, encourages, and comforts. Who is this? This is Jesus Christ. He was incarnated, passed through human living, died, resurrected, and ascended, and today He has come into us. This is too wonderful!

When He comes into us, we become His multiplication and

increase. What are Christians? Christians are people who have received the living Jesus into them to make them the duplication of Jesus. Therefore, we are His multiplication and His increase. In other words, we have become a part of Him; we have become members of His Body. Consider the four major limbs and the other hundreds of members in our body. Each member is a part of our body, that is, a part of us. We must realize that today we are a part of Christ. Individually we are His members, and corporately we are His Body. This Body is the church.

The church is the expression of Christ. I am expressed through my own body. If I did not have a body, if I were a spirit or a soul floating in the air, you could neither see nor touch me. Moreover, if you heard my speaking, you all would become frightened and run away. However, since I have a body to express me in an appropriate way, when I speak boldly, you can enjoy my speaking and not be the least bit afraid. Likewise, Christ needs a church to be His Body in this universe. His Body is not small as ours is; it is all-inclusive, and the believers in it are of all sorts of nationalities and races. It is also eternal and boundless; no one can count the number of the believers. It is needless to speak of those who have passed away; even the number of the living ones is hard to estimate. If today we arrive at a figure, by tomorrow morning another group of believers will be produced, and before we can finish counting them, still another group will be produced. Can we say how many people repent and believe in the Lord every day all over the globe? We cannot. For this reason the Body is eternal and boundless.

Dear brothers and sisters, you must definitely know that you should not be religionists. Rather, you must be included in Christ. You must be His multiplication and His increase. This is not merely to live for Jesus; this is to live as Jesus. To me, to live is Christ. I still exist, but this "I" has passed through death and has been resurrected.

CHAPTER FOUR

IN HIS RICHES AND FULLNESS

Scripture Reading: Col. 2:9; John 1:16; Eph. 3:8; John 16:15; Eph. 1:23; 4:13; 3:19b, 21

OUTLINE

I. All the fullness of the Godhead of the Triune God dwelling in Him bodily—Col. 2:9.

II. The fullness of the Godhead of the Triune God being the expression of the riches of the Triune God—John 1:16.

III. His unsearchable riches (Eph. 3:8) including all that the Father has (John 16:15), all that He is, and all that He has experienced and accomplished.

IV. By enjoying His riches we becoming His fullness—Eph. 1:23; 4:13.

V. His fullness being His Body as His expression, which is the fullness, the expression, of the Triune God—Eph. 3:19b.

VI. This fullness expressing the eternal and infinite Triune God eternally and infinitely—Eph. 3:21.

RICHES AND *FULLNESS* NOT BEING SYNONYMOUS

In this message we will consider the riches and fullness of Christ. The words *multiplication, increase, riches,* and *fullness* are all ordinary terms that are commonly heard. However, when these terms are placed in the exposition of the Bible, or rather in theology, they are not ordinary. Among the general teachers of the Bible and the theology that is generally taught, some of these words may never have been used, while others have been used without being understood. The two words *multiplication* and *increase* have never been used in ordinary theology. Not only in Chinese theology, but even in the theologies of the Western languages, such as Latin and English, it seems that *multiplication* and *increase* have not been used to describe the all-inclusiveness and unlimitedness of Christ. Although *riches* and *fullness* have been used, those who have been in Christianity for a considerable period of time may never have heard a single message or read a single book that preaches the riches of Christ. Many speak about the love of Christ and the grace of Christ, but I have yet to hear a message or read a book on the riches of Christ. Nevertheless, Paul said that he was commissioned by God to preach and announce the unsearchable riches of Christ as the gospel to the Gentiles. The gospel which Paul announced was not merely that Christ died on the cross for us to deal with our sin. Rather, it includes all the riches of Christ, and these riches are unsearchable. We thank God that even though we cannot fathom these riches, we can preach and enjoy them.

However, among Christians today, nearly no one pays attention to the riches of Christ. Everyone reads Ephesians; it is rare to find a genuine Christian who loves the Bible yet who has not spent much time studying Ephesians. The expression *the unsearchable riches of Christ* is in the book of Ephesians, yet people read it without paying attention to it, or they pay attention to it without comprehending it. It is a matter of fact that many Christians, even the brothers and sisters among us, are not adequate in their knowledge of the riches of Christ and even less adequate in their personal experience of the riches of Christ. Nonetheless, Paul spoke empathetically concerning this matter in Ephesians 3. He said, "To me, less than the least of all saints, was this grace given to announce to the Gentiles the unsearchable riches of Christ as the gospel" (v. 8). Thank the Lord that today we are the Gentile believers who are qualified to enjoy these riches!

What then of the term *fullness?* This is a troublesome term. I have been studying the books of Christianity for decades, and I have read a few on the fullness of Christ. Unfortunately, however, when people speak about *fullness,* they mostly consider it as a synonym of *riches.* To them, *riches* and *fullness* refer to the same thing—*riches* equals *fullness,* and *fullness* equals *riches.* This is so much the case that sometimes in contemporary Christian teachings and writings, the word *riches* is seldom used and the expression *the riches of Christ* is rarely mentioned. Rather, most people use the word *fullness,* but the fullness they speak of actually refers to the riches.

There are, of course, reasons for this. In the New Testament, the terms *riches* and *fullness* are used in such a deeply particular way that sometimes it is easy for people to have the understanding that *fullness* is *riches.* John 1:14 says, for example, "The Word became flesh and tabernacled among us..., full of grace and reality." If you look at the context here, how can you not understand that to be "full of" is to be "rich in"? We may change this sentence to: "The Word became flesh and tabernacled among us, rich in grace and reality." When you read this, you may not have the slightest sense that it is wrong. Then, in John 1:16, the Chinese version says, "For out of His full grace we have all received." If you read this in its context, His full grace obviously denotes His rich grace. It is no wonder almost all Christians understand the word *fullness* in the New Testament as a synonym of *riches,* thinking that *fullness* and *riches* refer to the same thing. However, it is not so in actuality. A great deal is involved here.

Thirty years ago when I had just come to Taiwan, I could not explain these two terms. I was puzzled about why there was *fullness* and there was also *riches,* wondering if they were indeed synonymous in the New Testament. However, after reading these passages repeatedly, I found out that they are not synonyms. In particular, when I read Ephesians 1:22b-23, which says, "The church, which is His Body, the fullness of the One who fills all in all," I saw that *church, Body,* and *fullness* are truly synonyms. The church is the Body, and the Body is the fullness. The church is the Body of Christ, and the Body of Christ is the fullness of Christ. But here it does not say "Christ"; instead, it says "the One who fills all in all." Therefore, in this verse there are three terms—the *church,* the *Body,* and the *fullness*—which all refer to the same thing—the church.

WHAT THE CHURCH IS

Of course, the church here is not the church as ordinarily understood by Christians today. In general, when Christians, especially in the West, speak of the church, they are referring to a chapel. When you see a chapel by the roadside, you may say that it is a church. When someone asks you, "Where is your church?" you may say, "Our church is on Chin Shan Street." Many people designate the church as the building where they meet. When we first came to Taiwan, we started to build the hall on Ren Ai Road. At first we built a small meeting hall with bricks and tiles. After about a year or two, it was too small to meet the need. So, we tore it down and changed it to a bigger meeting hall built with wood. I drew the design of the meeting hall, but after I handed it to the engineer, he looked at it and shook his head. He said, "This does not look like a church but a warehouse or storehouse. If you want to build a church, the ridge of the roof must be high, and there should be a bell tower either at the front or at the side. Then right away people can tell that it is a chapel." I have also seen religious pictures drawn by various Christians. When they represent the church, they usually draw a chapel with a steeple. Therefore, in the eyes of most Christians, a chapel is a church. This is truly a great error, even a great heresy.

The church is not a physical building but the Body of Christ. Please consider how a building can be the Body of Christ. Would you like to have a building as your body? Thus, you can see that what is generally taught, understood,

(Assembly) EKKlesia – the gathering together of the called[61] out ones .

and spoken in Christianity is far off the mark. For this reason, the Lord has a recovery. We cannot follow the traditions of Christianity. In the previous century, around the 1830s, the Lord raised up a group of brothers, who are referred to in history as the Brethren. When they were raised up, these brothers were full of light. Based upon the Bible, they told people that the church is by no means a physical building. What, then, is the church? They explained this according to the meaning of the Greek word. In Greek, the word for church is ekklesia, meaning a gathering together of the called-out ones. Therefore, when speaking about the church, the Brethren did not use the word church but the word assembly. Then after nearly seventy years, the Assembly of God was raised up out of a group of people in the Pentecostal movement in America. When they came to China to preach the gospel, they also did not use the word church but the word assembly. I believe that the term assembly is more accurate than the term church.

The Brethren said that the church is a group of people, chosen and redeemed by God, who have been called out by God to assemble together. This kind of exposition is much more advanced; it contains no error and is accurate. Nevertheless, this explanation has not hit home and is still too shallow. Today we are those who were chosen by God, and we have all been saved. Moreover, we have been called by God to assemble in our locality. This is the church in a true sense. However, if you have your flesh and opinions, I have my philosophy and views, and someone else has his preference and disposition, how can we get along in your flesh, in my philosophy, and in his preference when we come together? We will either argue or quarrel. Please consider this; when everyone is quarreling and arguing, is that the church? That is a flesh club, a quarrel club, and an argument club, but it is not the church. Yes, according to our standing, we are God's called-out ones and we are assembling as the people of the church. Nevertheless, according to the reality of the condition of life, this is not the church.

I have observed the conflict between the whites and the blacks in America. To this day no black person can come into certain Southern Baptist churches in the southern United States. A recent American president was a member of a Southern Baptist church. When he ran for office, he promised to give black people their proper position, and many black people gave him their votes. However, even he could not turn the situation around. That is why up to this day blacks and whites still have much conflict. You cannot say that the whites who believe in the Lord Jesus are not called by God, nor can you say that the blacks who believe in the Lord Jesus are not called by God. They are all called by God. However, when they come together, they are not the church because they are Christians in position only. In reality, they cannot say, "It is no longer I who live, but it is Christ who lives in me." If they all could say this, there would no longer be the distinction between whites and blacks. I simply say this much to show you the deformed situation of today's Christianity. It is so completely off the mark. Merely to say that the church is God's assembly, the gathering together of the called ones, is correct on the one hand and incorrect on the other hand. Do these called ones meet together by the Spirit and Christ, or do they meet in their mind, insight, perspective, preference, and disposition? If they come together according to their perspective, insight, disposition, and other traits, they are not the church.

ENJOYING THE RICHES OF CHRIST
TO BECOME HIS FULLNESS

I have spoken these things to show you what the church is. The church is the Body of Christ, which is the fullness of Christ. The measure of a person's stature is his fullness. A person with a short and slender stature does not appear healthy, but a tall and heavy person has a fullness. A large person is not born that way, but he gains his fullness by taking in food with its riches for many months and years. We have several thousands of brothers and sisters who are all called ones meeting together. We thank and praise the Lord that we neither quarrel nor argue. Rather, we all come to listen quietly to the Lord's word. Nevertheless, this is not the basis to determine the measure of the stature of Christ among us. Ephesians 4:13 says, "Until we all arrive...at the measure of the stature of the fullness of Christ." The fullness of Christ is the Body of Christ. Since it is the Body, there is a stature with a measure. Several thousand Christians who love the Lord may come together, but how much content, how much fullness of Christ, and how much measure of the stature of Christ do they have among them? This involves a great deal. We have been meeting together for many years, and unlike those who are outside the church, we do not wrangle or act loosely. This is a good situation that is commendable. However, how much stature of the Body of Christ does each one of us have within us? This is hard to say; it depends on how much Christ we have within. If each one of us is full of Christ within, each one lives Christ, and each can say, "I am crucified with Christ; and it is no longer I who live, but it is Christ who lives in me," then within we all have arrived at the full measure of the stature of the Body of Christ.

I believe that many of us have such an experience: Many times we regretted and repented not because we had done something wrong or committed a sin, but because we felt that we did not live by Christ that day. We may have said, "I am a good man, I love people, and I behave properly; everything about me is good, but I do not live by Christ." Do not think that those who do not live by Christ are devoid of goodness. There was a certain man in Chinese history named Liu Hsia-hwei who was said to have such great self-cultivation that he could retain his presence of mind in the face of extreme temptation. Wang Yang-ming, a great Confucius scholar of the Ming Dynasty, was also excellent in his self-control and self-cultivation. In his writings, some of which I have read, he said that one should not practice self-control merely as something outward, like trees without roots or springs without a source. He taught that one should work out something from within. I am convinced that his self-control was far better than what we see in the majority of Christians today. However, was that Christ? No matter how good it was, was it Christ? Wang Yang-ming could not say, "Now it is no longer I who live, but it is Christ who lives in me." We can say this, but he could not say this. Many times I have not done anything wrong for the whole day. I did not lose my temper but rather treated people with humility. Although I managed to do all these things for the whole day, at night before I went to bed I felt remorseful. I told the Lord, "O Lord, forgive me. Today everything about me was good, but I did not live you. Today I have had humility and patience, but I did not have Christ. In my living today, I did not live Christ." There is a big difference here.

Brothers and sisters, if one day you repent all the time not because you have sinned or done something wrong, but because you have done everything right without Christ, then I am convinced that at that time you will enter into a new stage in life. You will often pray, "Lord, forgive me. My living for the whole day was right but altogether without You. I did not live in spirit, I did not follow the Spirit, and I did not exercise to be one spirit with You. I was very good in being humble, patient, and loving, but I did not have You. I offended and contradicted You, and I even replaced and substituted You." I hope that you will have the experience of this stage.

Paul said, "For to me, to live is Christ" (Phil. 1:21a). Can you say that to you, to be patient, to be humble, to love your wife, or to submit to your husband is Christ? You cannot say that because it is altogether you, not Christ. Therefore, if we Christians truly love and pursue the Lord, we will reach a stage in which we feel that we lack Christ in our living and still have many replacements which replace Him. When you lose your temper, your temper may not replace Him, but when you endure by clenching your teeth, you may be replacing Christ.

Many years ago, a brother once invited several of us brothers to his home for a love feast. His wife, who had not yet received the Lord, was disgusted with his invitation. This brother worked in the customs office. Before he received the Lord, he used to take his wife out for pleasures and parties. Now that he was saved, his life had changed completely, and he loved to invite those of us who were co-workers and elders to have love feasts in his home. He may have overdone it somewhat, so his wife was very annoyed. That day I was among those invited, and I saw the situation myself. Once we brothers came into the house, we realized that something was wrong. He lived in a big house, and there were some beautiful paintings hanging on both sides of the hallway, but that day when we entered through the door, we saw that the paintings were on the floor. Right away we realized that this was a bad sign. The pictures did not fall by themselves; they had been struck down by his wife. Fortunately, his wife did not chase us away, so we went into the living room and sat down, and after sitting there for about half an hour, we went into the dining room to have the meal. To our surprise, the dishes and the rice on the table were all cold. The wife had served us with cold leftovers from the previous day. We looked at one another, not daring to say anything. We were worried that the brother would lose his temper and quarrel with his wife in front of us, and how embarrassing that would be! We looked to the Lord that He would "calm the wind and the sea" so that they would not fight in front of us. The brother was reluctant to pick up his chopsticks because he was so embarrassed, so we started eating in the hope that he would not say anything, and he joined us in eating. For him to endure such an insult and say nothing at that time was certainly something tremendous! I observed him and studied whether his enduring of the insult was out of himself or out of Christ. Later, I found the answer to my study. Half of it was Christ, but the other half was still himself, yet we thank and praise the Lord that we still saw a little of Christ there.

What is the church? The church is Christ. The church is the Body of Christ, which grows and is formed by the daily enjoyment of Christ, by us who belong to Him, through eating and drinking Him. This may be compared to our eating and drinking every day. The food and drink which we digest within us become the constituents of our body. When we enjoy the riches of Christ, we become the fullness of Christ.

WHAT THE RICHES OF CHRIST ARE

Now I want to speak a little on what the riches of Christ are. Today the pastors and preachers in Christianity mostly say that Christ, who is the Son of God, was incarnated, and because He loved sinners, He died for us on the cross, resurrected on the third day, and then ascended to heaven. What they say is right, but it does not give people the impression that Christ is rich and that His riches are unsearchable. Today's preaching in Christianity cannot give people this impression. Nonetheless, Paul's preaching gave people such an impression. We hope, by the mercy of the Lord, that the Lord's recovery also will give others this impression.

What, then, are the riches of Christ? In these years many brothers and sisters have been studying the New Testament and have all seen something. In the last two meetings, for example, we have covered what Christ is and what He has accomplished. What He is, is so rich. We can enumerate some of the items: He is God, the complete God—the Father, the Son, and the Spirit; He is the Triune God; He is Jehovah, the One who is without beginning and without end and who is self-existing and ever-existing; He is the great I Am. Jehovah is the I Am, and everything else in the universe is not. Temporarily, they are, but after a while, they are not; they exist only for today. He alone is the One who was, who is, and who will be. He is also the Creator, the omnipotent God. The word *God* in Hebrew is *Elohim,* meaning the almighty faithful One. In addition, He is the Angel of the Lord who is sent to take care of us. To a certain extent, we have experienced all these points.

Christ is also a man. This matter of His being a man is even more involved. As a man, He was conceived not of man but of the Holy Spirit. The Holy Spirit entered into the womb of the virgin Mary for this conception. Christ was born as a man with two natures, the divine nature and the human nature, because His conception involved both God and man. It was a great mystery that He possessed both divinity and humanity. This special person was a "Super-man." The blood He shed was human blood which qualified Him to make propitiation for our sins. Not only so, but since as God's Son He possessed divinity, the all-inclusiveness and unlimitedness of divinity became the efficacy of His blood. Therefore, His blood can redeem all people, and the redemption which He accomplished was an eternal and infinite redemption. If He were only a perfect man, His blood could redeem only one person, not billions of people, but since He is God, the eternal unlimitedness of God was within Him. Therefore, His blood became the eternal blood.

The riches of Christ also include the entire human living through which He passed. He said, "Come to Me all who toil and are burdened, and I will give you rest" (Matt. 11:28). How could He say such a word? It is because He, being meek and lowly, passed through human living. We can come to Him to take Him as life. When we enter into Him, the element of His human living becomes our element. This is also an item of His riches.

As we have already seen, His death was all-inclusive because when He died on the cross, He died with seven statuses. His death was a death not of only one aspect but of many aspects. When He died, He dealt with our sins, our sinful deeds; He dealt with our sin, our sinful nature; He destroyed Satan and nullified death; He dealt with the old man; He terminated the old creation; and He abolished all the different practices, customs, and ordinances among people. In addition, on the positive side, when He died, He released the divine life within Him from the shell of His humanity. By this we can see that His death was an all-inclusive death, and we can enjoy His death. The death of Christ preached to us by most Christians seems to have only one aspect, that is, that He was crucified for our sins and punished by God on our behalf that we may not suffer an eternal penalty. However, according to the revelation of the Bible, the death of Christ is rich with many aspects.

Christ also resurrected. This does not mean that He lay in the tomb, slept for three days, and then suddenly came out of Hades, as we formerly may have understood it to mean. This is not what resurrection means. If you study the Bible thoroughly, you will see that when He was nailed on the cross and dying there, His Spirit within was activated. This is like a grain of wheat which is sown into the ground. While its shell is decaying in the soil, the life within it is activated and begins to grow. When Christ was dying on the cross, His body passed through death and His Spirit within became operative. On the third day, He did not escape from death; rather,

He lived and grew out of death. His resurrection was also His work and power. We often have problems, burdens, and sufferings, but we pray much, and the more we pray, the more we get into the Spirit, and the more we get into the Spirit, the more we touch Christ. This Christ within us has the effect both of death and of resurrection. This is our enjoyment of both His death and His resurrection.

Furthermore, He ascended. We cannot exhaust our speaking concerning all these aspects. In Ephesians 3 Paul seemed to be saying, "I, Paul, have been given the grace and have received a ministry to announce to you the unsearchable riches of Christ. I neither announce Judaism nor announce the Old Testament to you, but I announce to you Christ as a living person. He was God yet man, and He was also man yet God. He was the One who created and redeemed; He became flesh and passed through human living. He entered into death and in His death He did various works. He also resurrected, and in His resurrection He accomplished a further exceedingly great work. All these are the elements of His riches."

The Gospel of John speaks many items of Christ as the I Am: I am the life, I am the light, I am the bread of life, I am the door, I am the green pasture, I am the good Shepherd, and I am the Lamb of God. In 1 Corinthians, there are also numerous items of what Christ is, such as God's wisdom, God's righteousness, God's sanctification, God's power, the depths (deep things) of God, our food, our living water, the last Adam, the second man, and the life-giving Spirit in resurrection.

ENJOYING THE RICHES OF CHRIST BY PRAY-READING THE WORD AND PRAYING INTO THE SPIRIT

Christ is the life-giving Spirit. Where is He today? On the one hand, He is the Lord and Christ on the throne in heaven, while on the other hand, He is the life-giving Spirit who has entered into us to be our life. No matter how rich the food and water we need are, if they do not get into our stomach, they still have nothing to do with us. Today Christ is not only the Lord of all on the throne in heaven, but also the real and living life-giving Spirit indwelling our spirit to be our life. How good and how wonderful this is!

Unfortunately, Christians today have been separated from Christ by many things. It is needless to speak of sin and the world, for even reading the Bible may separate you from Christ. This is because in reading the Bible, you may only use your mind to study and not use your spirit to pray over the words of life. For example, you may read Matthew 1:1, which says, "The book of the generation of Jesus Christ, the son of David, the son of Abraham." When you come to the name of Abraham, you may be puzzled; you may not understand what the meaning of Abraham is. When I was young, I encountered this problem. I tried my best to search through the dictionaries, Bible encyclopedias, concordances, and the like. I was fully disappointed even when I found the explanation. I found an entry that said that Abraham was the father of Isaac. Who then is Isaac? I still did not understand. Therefore, I often wasted my time. I studied the Bible for an hour and a half in the morning, and the result was that my head was spinning. I would have been better off not reading the Bible. If I would have instead prayed a few sentences, I could at least have touched the Spirit to some degree. Because of the way I studied the Bible, I was farther away from God than when I first started. I tried to study Matthew 1, but the record of the genealogy, which goes all the way to verse 17 and contains many strange names, befuddled me. In addition, verse 17 mentions three ages of fourteen generations each. All the generations from Abraham until David were fourteen generations, from David until the deportation to Babylon were fourteen generations, and from the deportation to Babylon until the Christ were fourteen generations. I began to count the three ages of fourteen generations. However, no matter how I counted, I could not get it right. In the end, I was completely confused. Thereafter, I said, "Forget about it! There is no way to study the first seventeen verses in Matthew 1." That was why in the first few years, every time I read Matthew, I always started from verse 18.

Sometimes reading the Bible with the mind can also be satisfying. As a young person you may be saved and stirred up to love the Lord, and your heart may fully desire to honor your parents, to be diligent, and to do things single-heartedly.

The Bible contains many such words, and when you read them, you feel very comfortable and satisfied. When sisters first read the Bible and come to the verse in Ephesians 5 which says that the husbands should love their wives, everyone who is a wife smiles and nods her head. To her, this Bible is very good and is the best book. This is because there is no wife who does not expect her husband to love her. The words in the Bible simply match what your heart loves. Conversely, the brothers enjoy reading the verse in Ephesians 5 which says that the wives should be subject to their husbands. This is truly good, because what the husbands daily hope for is that their wives would be subject to them.

Of the two kinds of sensations in reading the Bible, as illustrated above, one is very dry and puzzling, and the other is very interesting and satisfying. These two seem to be entirely different, but both separate you from the enjoyment of Christ. We need to see that the Bible was not written for this purpose. The Bible is God's words, and God's words are spirit. The Lord Jesus said, "The words which I have spoken to you are spirit and are life" (John 6:63b). Every sentence in the Bible is spirit and life. No matter whether you are old or young, learned or unlearned, I would suggest that you do not skip Matthew 1:1-17 but rather read every verse. When you read "Abraham begot Isaac, and Isaac begot Jacob," even though you do not understand it, do not try to understand it. One day you will understand, and that will be the real understanding. You should simply pray-read, "The book of the generation of Jesus Christ, the son of David, the son of Abraham: Abraham begot Isaac, and Isaac begot Jacob, and Jacob begot Judah and his brothers." Do not care whether or not you understand; simply pray-read, and you will inwardly touch the Spirit. Facts speak louder than words. Try and pray-read, and see which of these two ways of reading the Bible supplies you more. I do not have to pray-read for half an hour; I can be enlivened by pray-reading for only five minutes.

Our Lord is rich today. He was the eternal God, the Creator, and the One who rules over the whole universe, upholding and bearing all things by the word of His power. One day, He came to be incarnated. He entered into the womb of a virgin and was willing to be born as a man. He passed through human living for over thirty-three years, experiencing all kinds of hardships and tasting all sorts of joys and sorrows. Then He entered into death, and He did great things in His death, accomplishing one thing after another. Sins were removed, sin was dealt with, all things were ended, and the divine life was released. Then He entered into resurrection, and He regenerated us in His resurrection. He also became the life-giving Spirit to enter into us today. Not only so, He ascended to the throne. The indwelling Christ in us today is also the Christ sitting on the throne. All these are His riches.

The most central point is that He is the Spirit, even the life-giving Spirit. This Spirit is in God's word and in your spirit. Whenever you open your mouth to pray, you can touch this Spirit. Therefore, all of us need to pray. You must pray, and you must also pray-read the Bible. Daily you need to contact this Spirit, be filled with this Spirit, and let this Spirit operate within you to saturate you. Dear brothers and sisters, if you experience this, you will enjoy the unsearchable riches of Christ.

We all have our husbands, wives, children, families, and careers; we all have burdens and hardships. All these are ordained by God, for this is our human life. How do we handle all these matters? It is extremely difficult to handle them by ourselves, so we must depend on the Lord. Paul told us in Philippians 1:19 that the bountiful supply of the Spirit of Jesus Christ enables us to enjoy salvation in our living. To obtain the supply of this Spirit, we must pray, because this Spirit can be contacted only by our spirit. Whenever we contact this Spirit, He will supply, saturate, permeate, and water us. This Spirit is Jesus Christ, the Triune God, the One who is both God and man, and the all-inclusive Spirit. If you enjoy Him daily in such a way, you will enjoy His riches.

BECOMING THE FULLNESS OF CHRIST AFTER HAVING ENJOYED HIS RICHES

When we thus enjoy the riches of Christ, we will be filled by Christ. You are full of Christ, I am full of Christ, and we all are full of Christ. As a result, when we come together, we are His Body, which is the fullness of the One who fills all in all. This fullness is His expression. A glass may contain water, but if the glass is not full, the water will not overflow. If you add more and more water until the glass is so full that the water overflows, this is fullness. The overflowing of the water is the fullness of the water. This fullness expresses the water for people to see.

Today Christ wants to fill us. He is the Spirit, and as such, He wants to fill us until He overflows from within us. This overflowing is the fullness, and this fullness is His expression, which is the church. The church is the expression of Christ. Furthermore, since Christ is God, the church is also the fullness, the expression, of God. I hope that you can see that in the riches of Christ there is His all-inclusiveness, and in the fullness of Christ there is His unlimitedness. The all-inclusiveness and the unlimitedness of Christ are manifested in His riches and in His fullness. The manifestation of His riches and His fullness hinges on our enjoyment of Him. The more we enjoy Him, and the more we experience Him together with the saints in the church, the more we express His all-inclusiveness. We thank and praise the Lord that today He wants to recover this. You cannot be a superficial Christian "skating on the ice" according to the pattern of today's Christianity. You must not be like this. You must be a deep Christian. You need to pray, read the Bible, and enter into the Bible. Break the ice and get into the depths of the water to probe the riches in it. When we experience Christ, we enjoy His riches, and as a result, we become His fullness. Thank and praise Him for this!

CHAPTER FIVE

IN HIS LIVING OUT AND TESTIMONY

Scripture Reading: 1 Pet. 1:3; Eph. 2:6; 1 Cor. 15:45b; Gal.
2:20a; 2 Tim. 4:22; Phil. 1:19-21a; Acts 1:8; Rev. 1:9; 21:2, 10;
22:5b

OUTLINE

I. In His multiplying resurrection (1 Pet. 1:3; Eph. 2:6)
He becoming the all-inclusive life-giving Spirit—
1 Cor. 15:45b.

II. This all-inclusive life-giving Spirit dwelling and
living in the countless members whom He has regenerated—Gal. 2:20a; 2 Tim. 4:22.

III. We living Him out by the bountiful supply of this all-
inclusive life-giving Spirit (Phil. 1:19-21a) as His wit-
nesses and testimony—Acts 1:8; Rev. 1:9.

IV. This testimony being universal and spreading to the
uttermost part of the earth—Acts 1:8.

V. The ultimate consummation of this testimony being
the New Jerusalem, which is eternal, full, and end-
less—Rev. 21:2, 10; 22:5b.

In this message we will see how the all-inclusiveness and unlimitedness of Christ can be seen in our living and testimony. We live out and testify Christ, and in such a living out and testimony Christ is all-inclusive and unlimited.

WE BEING ALL-INCLUSIVE IN OUR LIVING ONLY BY LIVING OUT CHRIST

People have problems because they are not inclusive. Once again we may use husbands and wives as an illustration. Many of you are married. Please tell me, is there inclusiveness between you and your husband or wife? Are you inclusive with your wife? Are you inclusive with your husband? If you are willing to speak an honest word, you will admit that no one is inclusive. Nevertheless, when your experience of life reaches an extent in which you can truly say, "It is no longer I who live, but it is Christ who lives in me," then you are inclusive. The reason why couples are separated or divorced is that they are not inclusive. Sometimes the husband thinks that his wife is a burden to him and he has no way to be inclusive with her. Sometimes the wife also feels that her husband is too annoying and she has no way to be inclusive with him. Why are you not inclusive? It is because you are not the multiplication of Christ. If you can truly say, "I am crucified with Christ, and it is no longer I who live," then you are inclusive, and your inclusiveness is unlimited. The truths that we have released in these messages are not empty doctrines but can be put into practice in spirit. If you can say, "O Lord, I am crucified with You, and it is no longer I who live," then you will have no problem getting along in the church with ninety thousand brothers and sisters, let alone nine thousand. You will be able to be inclusive with everyone.

In the churches, I often come across brothers and sisters who come to me with their problems. In America, sometimes some brothers who are overseas Chinese have come to me, saying, "Brother Lee, we can't stand a certain American brother. His American flavor is too strong." In less than two weeks' time, an American brother may also come, saying, "Brother Lee, how can this be? Those Chinese brothers bear too much of the Chinese flavor!" We can see from this that when we live in our self, there is no way for us to be inclusive. We must see and realize that we are the multiplication of Christ. "It is no longer I who live, but it is Christ who lives in me." Whenever we live by Christ, we live out His all-inclusiveness.

ENJOYING THE INCLUSIVENESS AND UNLIMITEDNESS OF CHRIST BY THE BOUNTIFUL SUPPLY OF THE SPIRIT OF JESUS CHRIST

The apostle Paul wrote the book of Philippians during his imprisonment in Rome. He was mistreated there and may have expected to be martyred soon. However, he said in Philippians 1:19 that he knew that his suffering would turn out for him to salvation because of the bountiful supply of the Spirit of Jesus Christ. Paul was not preaching ethics or morality; what he preached was the bountiful supply of the Spirit of Jesus Christ. The Spirit of Jesus Christ is not only the Spirit of God but also the Spirit of Jesus and the Spirit of Christ. This Spirit has a bountiful supply. This bountiful supply, which is all-inclusive and unlimited, enables us to endure what others cannot endure and to bear what others cannot bear.

In Ephesians 3:17 Paul said, "That Christ may make His home in your hearts." *Make...home* here is a strong word. When Christ makes His home in our entire being, we can experience the breadth, length, height, and depth of the universe. What is the breadth? What is the length? What is the height? What is the depth? It is hard to say. How deep is to be deep? How high is to be high? Paul indicated that the breadth, length, height, and depth of the universe is Christ. Christ is the boundless dimensions of the universe. This is why Paul said that the Lord's riches are unsearchable as the breadth, length, height, and depth. Paul experienced Christ to an extent that he reached the boundless dimensions of the universe. Thus, he knew that Christ's endurance, love, power, and wisdom are unlimited, and everything of Christ is boundless. He knew from experience that when we become His multiplication and increase and thereby experience Him, we will realize that our Lord is infinite. Christ is all-inclusive and unlimited.

ALL SPIRITUAL EXPERIENCES HINGING ON THIS SPIRIT

This experience altogether depends on the Spirit. The operation of electrical appliances, such as light bulbs, radios, microphones, televisions, audio and video tape recorders, and even computers, hinges on electricity. Once the electricity is cut off, all the electrical appliances stop their operation. All Christians' experiences of multiplication and increase depend on the bountiful supply of the Spirit of Jesus Christ. Brothers and sisters, the vision we have seen by the Lord's grace is that this Spirit is the key to all our spiritual experiences. It is not doctrines, religion, history, or any trend, but this all-inclusive and infinite Christ. This Christ today is the Spirit, the all-inclusive Spirit. What is the reality of the church? When we live in this Spirit, and when this Spirit flows out of us, we are the reality of the church. When this reality is expressed in a locality, this expression is the local church. Universally speaking, it is the universal church, which is the Body of Christ.

THE SEVEN SPIRITS OPERATING IN MANY WAYS TO MAKE US THE MULTIPLICATION AND INCREASE OF CHRIST

Now this all-inclusive Christ is still here. He is sent as the seven Spirits to all the earth, working in us in many ways to make us, one by one, His duplication, multiplication, and increase. Eventually, at His coming, there will be the manifestation of the kingdom, and the ultimate manifestation will be the New Jerusalem. This is His testimony. We are His multiplication and increase, and when we live in this multiplication and increase, we become His testimony. This testimony grows and increases day by day, first as the church, then as the kingdom, and lastly as the New Jerusalem in the new heaven and new earth.

May the Lord open our eyes and save us from our traditional and religious perspectives. In actuality we are not Christianity; rather, we are Christ. This living Christ who is in us makes us who believe in Him His multiplication and increase. To us, to live is Him; hence, we are His testimony. This testimony is not only individual but also corporate. First it is the church, then it is the kingdom, and lastly it is the New Jerusalem in the new heaven and new earth.